"'He had a knack, which was his lure, for both the mundane and fantastic'—so says John D'Agata about one of his book's eccentric population, but he could be describing his own omnivorous self. His writing is marked by an exuberance of structural invention, by an ever-churning hurdy-gurdy lexicon of lingual play, and by citizenship in the mazes of the mind and in hallways that mimic *Ripley's Believe It Or Not*. Or, to update that last comparison: *Halls of Fame* is to essays what the Museum of Jurassic Technology is to gallery dioramas." —Albert Goldbarth

"D'Agata writes masterful sentences, in all forms. Adept at collage, found poetry, paragraphs long and short, lists, characterization, direct quotes, the prose poem, fragments, spoofing, and a perceptiveness that sometimes only dispassionate description can achieve, D'Agata hovers like a moth around the sparks created where the known and the unknown rub against each other." —*Ruminator Review*

"With the diligence of a manic tour guide, D'Agata exhaustively catalogues his encounters, inventing whole new ways of looking as he goes." —*Rain Taxi*

"The dialectic between showing and looking, between telling and knowing, is D'Agata's subject and his supremacy; these lyric essays result in further questions, for such a process does not 'lead' to mere answers; when such prodigies of mystery as Henry Darger or Martha Graham are at issue, this turn of mind, this trope of thinking, is a revelation; that is the discursive poet's program: *to reveal*, and indeed his progress through the generality of our native offerings is a triumphant one; not since Butor's *Mobile* have I learned so much about America's creases and crannies, such learning being a complexion of pains and pleasures." —Richard Howard

Halls of Fame

ESSAYS BY

John D'Agata

Graywolf Press
SAINT PAUL, MINNESOTA

Publication of this volume is made possible in part by a grant provided by the
Minnesota State Arts Board through an appropriation by the Minnesota State
Legislature, and by a grant from the National Endowment for the Arts. Significant
support has also been provided by the Bush Foundation; Dayton's Project Imagine
with support from Target Foundation; the McKnight Foundation; a Grant made
on behalf of the Stargazer Foundation; and other generous contributions from
foundations, corporations, and individuals. To these organizations and
individuals we offer our heartfelt thanks.

September 29, 1995 AP article.
Reprinted with permission of The Associated Press.

Excerpts from *The Flat Earth News* articles #54 (1985) and #87 (1993)
are reprinted with the permission of Charles Johnson.

All best efforts have been made to obtain permission from the Darger estate
for the excerpts from Henry Darger's unpublished novel.

Excerpts from the Deep Springs *Alumni Newsletter,* Vol. 64, No. 1, Fall 1997,
are reprinted with permission.

Published by Graywolf Press
2402 University Avenue, Suite 203
Saint Paul, Minnesota 55114
All rights reserved.

www.graywolfpress.org

Published in the United States of America

ISBN 1-55597-314-0 (cloth)
ISBN 1-55597-377-9 (paper)

2 4 6 8 9 7 5 3 1

Library of Congress Catalog Card Number: 00-101780

Cover design: Scott Sorenson
Cover art: Woody Gwyn, *Highway 1,* oil on canvas, 24 × 168, 1991–1992

For Dougie

Contents

The halls of fame are open wide
and they are always full;
some go in by the door called push
and some by the door called pull.

ANONYMOUS

Door No. One

The Wonders of the Abacus; The Wonders of Accounting; The Wonders of Acoustics; The Wonders of the Age: Masterpieces of Early Safavid Painting, 1501–1576; The Wonders of Alaska; The Wonders of Algae; The Wonders of Alligators and Crocodiles; The Wonders of Ancient Chinese Science; The Wonders of Animal Architecture; The Wonders of Animal Disguises; The Wonders of Animal Ingenuity: By Famous Writers of Natural History; Ant Hill Wonders; The Wonders of the Antarctic; The Wonders of the Approaching End; The Wonders of Astronomy; The Wonders of the Atmosphere; The Wonders of the Air: The Trembling of the Earth.

Round Trip

I

Isaac, who is twelve, has come involuntarily.

"We insist he grow up cultured," his mother says, leaning over our headrests from the seat behind. "My father brought me to Hoover Dam on a bus. There is just no other way to see it."

Hours ago, before the bus, I found the tour among the dozens of brochures in my hotel lobby. It had been typed and Xeroxed, folded three times into the form of a leaflet, and crammed into the back of a countertop rack on the bellhop's "What To Do" desk in Vegas.

Nearby my tour in the brochure rack were announcements for Colorado River raft rides that would paddle visitors upstream into the great gleaming basin of the dam.

There were ads, too, for helicopter rides—offering to fly "FOUR friends and YOU" over "CROWDS, TRAFFIC, this RIVER & MAN's MOST BEAUTIFUL structure—all YOURS to be PHOTOGRAPHED at 10,000 FEET!"

Hot-air balloon tours.

Rides on mountain bikes.

Jaunts on donkeys through the desert, along the river, and up the dam's canyon wall.

There was even something called the Hoover Dam Shopper's Coach, whose brochure guaranteed the best mall bargains in Nevada, yet failed to mention anywhere on its itinerary Hoover Dam.

Brochure in hand, I stood in line at the tour's ticket booth behind a man haggling with a woman behind the glass. He wanted a one-way ticket to Hoover Dam.

"Impossible," the woman said. "We sell The Eleven-Dollar Tour. One tour, one price."

The one-way man went on about important business he had at the dam, things he had to see to, how the tour's schedule just wasn't time enough.

"Sir," she said, through security glass, "I'm telling you, you'll have to come back. They're not gonna let you stay out there."

He bought a ticket, moved on.

We boarded.

Like the ad said, The Eleven-Dollar Tour comes with a seat on the bus, a free hot-dog coupon, and a six-hour narrative, there and back.

Our bus is silver, round, a short, chubby thing. It is shaped like a bread box. Like a bullet. "Like they used to make them," says Isaac's mom.

I turn to Isaac, my seatmate, say, "Hi, my name is John," and he says he doesn't care, and proceeds to pluck the long blond lashes from his eyelids, one by one, standing them on his wrist, stuck there by their follicles.

It is at this point that Isaac's mom leans over our headrests and tells me that Isaac is a good boy, "talkative, really," that he just happens to be grumpy today because "Mother and Father" have insisted that he accompany them on this "educational tour." Isaac's mother tells me that to keep Isaac entertained in Las Vegas they are staying in a new hotel—the largest in the world, in fact—with 5,000 guest rooms, 4 casinos, 17 restaurants, a mega-musical amphitheater, a boxing ring, a monorail, and a 33-acre amusement park, all inside an emerald building. She presents the brochure.

I say, "Wow."

Then Isaac's dad, looking up from another brochure he holds in his lap, says, "You know, kiddo, this Hoover Dam looks pretty special!" And then come statistics from the paragraph he's reading.

The feet high.

The feet thick.

The cubic yards of concrete.

Of water.

The 3 million kilowatts.

And the plaque.

"Let me see that." Isaac's mom takes the brochure and reads the plaque's inscription to herself. She shakes her head.

"Do you believe that? Isaac, honey, listen."

Isaac's eyes roll far away. His mother's voice climbs up a stage.

She is just loud enough to be overheard. Just hushed enough to silence all of us.

It is her voice, and the quiet, and the words on the plaque that I think might have made the whole trip worth it even then, even before we left the tour company's parking lot and learned there'd be no air-conditioning on the six-hour ride; even before we stood in line for two hours at the dam; before the snack bar ran out of hot dogs and the tour guide of his jokes; before the plaque was laid in 1955 by Ike; before the dam was dedicated in 1935 by FDR; before the ninety-six men died "to make the desert bloom"; or before the Colorado first flooded, before it leaked down from mountains, carved the Grand Canyon, and emptied into the ocean. Even before this plaque was cast by a father and his son in their Utah blacksmith shop, there was the anticipation of the plaque, its gold letters riding on the backs of all creators. And Isaac's mother's voice, even then, I believe, was ringing circles somewhere in the air: ". . . the American Society of Civil Engineers voted this one of the Seven Modern Wonders of the World!"

> *These are the seven wonders of the world: a beacon, a statue, gardens, pyramids, a temple, another statue, and a tomb. I have set eyes on them all—this Lofty fire of Pharos, and the statue of Zeus by Alpheus, and the Hanging Gardens, and the Colossus of the Sun, and the Huge Labor of the High Pyramids, and the Vast tomb of Mausolus, and the House of Artemis mounted to the Clouds—and I tell you, as a scholar and as a wanderer and as a man devoted to the gods, they are and always will be the Seven Greatest Liberties man will ever take with Nature.*
>
> (Antipater of Sidon, from his lost guidebook, c. 120 B.C.)

Our driver maneuvers lithely through the streets filled with rental cars. I tilt my head into the aisle. There is his green-sleeved arm, his pale, pudgy hand that is dancing on the gear stick rising out of the floor. His head, bobbing above the rows of seats in front of me, seems to bounce in rhythm with his horn. He honks to *let* pedestrians cross.

He rearranges his hair.

Leans a little forward.

Fluffs a cushion at his back.

We are idling at a crosswalk. We are there seven minutes, when suddenly, out of the air, our driver's voice comes coiling.

On the right side of us is the Flamingo Hotel where Elvis Presley owned a floor of that hotel on our right side.

On the left side of us is the Mirage Hotel where Michael Jackson owns a floor of that hotel on our left side.

His words emit circles, whip bubbles around our heads. His sentences wrap around the bus and greet themselves in midair. All the way to the dam the bus rumbles inside this cloud, the date slips steadily away, the tour transforms into a silent scratchy film that is slowly flitting backward through frames of older dreams.

We sit among neo-Gothic images heaping up from the pages of a souvenir borrowed from Isaac's grandfather, a 1935 photographic essay entitled "The Last Wonder of the World: The Glory of Hoover Dam." On its brittle pages machines still throb, light still beams from the book's center spread.

A full, glossy, long-shot view of the generator room reveals round, sleek, plastic bodies lined up like an army, surrounded by looming concrete walls adorned with pipes of gleaming chrome. Everything stands at attention. Nothing but light is stirring. The whole scene is poised forever to strike against an enemy that never breached the river's shore.

Gambling wasn't legalized in our state until 1935 is when they legalized gambling in Nevada.

The patterns in these pictures are like wax dripping from candles, islands coagulating from spurts of lava, liquid steel pouring out of kettles into rifle molds, Buick frames, the skyscrapers of Chicago. The round machines spin their energy like spools, all of it rolling off their bodies, through the pages, over the slick, curved surface of the next machine, which is identical to the last: which is blinking the same, rounded the same, parodying his sentences revolving around our heads, and shielding our tour from starts and stops, from *In the beginning,* from *Ever after,* from *Now* and from *Then,* and from any time—from all time—in which this vacuous progression cannot fit, because its round body is nowhere near the right shape for the boxy borders of dates.

Just to let you know, folks, our tour company's been on the road since 1945 is how long we've been traveling this road.

I mention to Isaac that the machines resemble something I once saw in *Doctor Who,* and he says, "No they don't"—which is the first thing he has said to me in an hour.

"It's more like *Star Trek*'s Plasma Generator," he says. But when I tell him I don't quite follow him, we decide that something from *Batman* suits our conflicting descriptions best.

What we do not know at this moment, however, is that in

1935, when the dam was opened, Batman was about to make his debut in comic strips. So was Superman, and other super-heroes—summoned from Krypton or Gotham City to defend our country against impending evils—their bodies toned flawlessly as turbines. They came with tales of an ideal Tomor row. They came jostled between two wars, buffering our borders against enemies on every side, encircling the country with an impenetrable force field, and introducing at home a new architecture of resistance: round, sleek, something the old clunky world slipped off.

A lot of these trees and most of this grass is brought in from out of state.

A lot of these trees and most of this grass is brought in from Arizona.

These are the same curves I once found in my grand-mother's basement. Toasters so streamlined they're liable to skid off the kitchen counter. A hair dryer filched from Frank-enstein's brain-wave lab. A Philharmonic radio taller than my ten-year-old body, and reeking of Swing—leaking tinny voices, platinum songs, and the catch-me-if-you-can whorls from Benny Goodman's silvery tube.

My grandmother's is the world that dropped the bomb—itself a slick object—so elegantly smooth it managed to slip past American consciousness, past enemy lines.

Afterward, in her world, "Atomic" was a prefix attached to the coming world and all the baubles to be found there. But in that present, at the opening of Hoover Dam, the designers of the future could only have guessed what atoms looked like.

And still their imaginations leaped instantly to *round,* to *fast,* to *heralds of the future.*

3

During the sixth century, St. Gregory of Tours com-
piled a list of the seven wonders of the medieval world
which demonstrates an inaccurate knowledge of his-
tory. He retained four wonders from the original list,
but made three additions of his own: Noah's Ark,
Solomon's Temple, and the Original Tree of Life—
which, he claimed, had been discovered in the under-
ground archives of a church in his native France. But
St. Gregory, of course, was wrong. The remains of the
Tree of Life were used to construct the Crucifix on
which our Saviour died—now housed, of course, in
the Holy Cross Church in Rome.

(from my grandmother's library, G. B. Smith's *Remem-*
bering the Saints)

4

"There's this computer game I like so I guess that counts right? It's not the real world but it lets you do really awesome stuff that's pretty cool so you can call that a wonder I bet. But I gotta go to my friend's house to play it though 'cause my parents won't get it for me 'cause they think it's too violent. Hey you can't write this down or I'm not talking man. It's called

Civilization. You start with two guys—a guy and a girl—and they're like at the start of the world or something. But after all the animals are made and stuff. And then—um—you have to make babies because the whole point is to you know start the civilization. So the computer keeps asking you what you want to do. Like if you want to have babies at a certain time or if you wanna be a hunter and gatherer or start farming and all that. So at the same time the computer has its own family that it's starting and you have to be in competition with them. So you start your family and all that and you become a village and . . . that's all the boring stuff. But you have to do it to start up the game. So before you know it you're like the leader and everything and people start gods and that kind of stuff and there's laws that you get to make up like if you want people to steal or how many wives you can have. And all of a sudden the computer calls war on you and you have to fight them 'cause if you don't then the game ends 'cause the computer can kill all your people. So there's whole long parts when you gotta learn how to do battle and you decide if you wanna use your metal to make weapons or not and how many people you'll make fight 'cause after you play a long time you learn that if you keep some people in the village during the war you can make them keep making weapons and stuff and help the fighters who are hurt. And usually if you make it through the war with some people left then the computer won't kill you off 'cause it'll let you try to start the village again. So all that happens and—um—every now and then the computer lets you know that someone in the village makes an invention. Like if they use the well to try to make a clock or they build a building with stones that has a roof so you can put more floors on top of it and—you know—then cities start. Then people start sailing down the river and they find other places to live and there are like whole new civilizations that the computer controls that you get to find. Now it all depends on how you act with the new people that tells whether or not you start a war or something or if you join their village and team up your forces. When that happens the computer gives you a lot more technology. So all that goes on and like thousands of years go by and pretty soon it starts looking like the modern world and you're controlling a whole country. Then your goal is to get control of the whole world which only one of my friends has done but then there's always this little place you don't know about that starts a revolution and then the whole world starts fighting and everyone ends up dead. I've never gotten that far though. I've controlled a couple countries before and I usually make them all start a colony in space and what's great is that if you tell them to fly to a planet in the solar system then the computer isn't programmed that far and it lets you do whatever you want for a little while until it just ends the game 'cause it doesn't know how to continue 'cause it can't compete with you if you just keep inventing new stuff it hasn't heard of. So sometimes I get like three countries to go up there and they start this whole new civilization and there are new animals and just the right amount of people and all the buildings are beautiful and built with this river that turns hard when you pick up the water and you can shape it how you want. So there's all this glass around and it's awesome but it only lasts like a year because the computer gets freaked out and ends up stopping the game. The game always ends up destroying the world."

5

When the Canal was being completed, the renowned sculptor Daniel Chester French and the best-known landscape architect of the day, Frederick Law Olmsted, were hired to decorate it. After a careful survey, the two artists refused the commission. So impressed were they by the beauty which the engineers had created that they declared, "For we artists to add to it now would be an impertinence."

1. The Panama Canal, 1914

My List

"Hello, Joe Miller here."

"Hi, sir. I'm wondering if maybe you could help me out. I'm trying to find the American Society of Civil Engineers' list of the Seven Modern Wonders of the World. Are you the right person to talk to?"

"Yeah, yeah that's me. I think the list you're talking about is pretty old, though. We just announced a new list you might be interested in."

"A new list?"

"The 1999 Modern Wonders of the World."

"Oh. Well, actually I guess I'm interested in the old Modern list."

"Well that's forty years old! This new one we have is a lot more impressive. I think this is what you're looking for."

"Well, could you maybe tell me about the first list anyway? I can't find it mentioned anywhere in my library. I kind of need it."

"Well, that'll take some time. . . . Let me get back to you . . ."

A common witticism on that bleak Depression day when this spectacular skyscraper opened its doors was, "The only way the landlords will ever fill that thing is if they tow it out to sea." But such pessimistic sentiments were wrong, as pessimists always have been in America. The population of the building now is that of a small city!

2. The Empire State Building,
1931

MY GRANDFATHER'S LIST

"Just put down the Statue of Liberty.
That's all I want you to put down."

How do you dig a hole deeper than anyone has ever dug, fill it with more concrete and steel than has been used in any other public works campaign, and do it all in the middle of California's

busiest harbor, swiftest current, most stormy shore? No, no! it
would be sheer folly to try—but they did it anyway!

> 3. The San Francisco–Oakland Bay
> Bridge, 1936

My Mother's List

1. The Twin Towers
2. The Apollo Space Program
3. PCs
4. Cannabis
5. Picasso
6. August 9, 1974 (Richard Nixon's resignation)
7. Cape Cod

Then the fun begins. The aqueduct's route crosses two hundred
forty-two miles of terrain that looks as if it had been dropped in-
tact from the moon: a landscape of mountainous sands, dry
washes, empty basins—one of the hottest, deadliest wastelands in
the civilized world. . . . And this conduit, man's longest, spans it
all!

> 4. The Colorado River Aque-
> duct, 1938

Isaac's Mother's List

"Oh, I know these. One must be the Brooklyn
Bridge. I practically grew up on that thing! The

Eiffel Tower has to be on there. Probably the Sears Tower, too. The Washington Monument. Niagara Falls. What about the Pentagon? And the Hoover Dam, of course."

Flying over the city, below the left wing of the plane, you will see Chicago's Southwest Works, one of the largest and most advanced sewage treatment facilities in the world. It is a veritable modern city, as spanking-looking as if sealed in a fresh-washed bottle, and as motionless and silent as a hospital at night.

5. The Chicago Sewage Disposal System, 1939

Guy-in-a-bar's List

1. A rapid development in our fine and visual arts
2. With all of our technological advancements, a continued sadness among the people
3. Our ignorance of environmental problems
4. Magic
5. The Internet
6. Alaska
7. Hoover Dam

A certain stopper was the fact that the Coulee could only rise to 550 feet. At that height it backed up the Columbia River into a 150-mile-long lake. Any higher and it would have flooded Canada.

6. The Grand Coulee Dam, 1941

"Yeah, this is a message for John D'Agata. I have that information you requested. This is the 1999 list of Modern Wonders of the World:

> one is The Golden Gate Bridge;
> two, The World Trade Center;
> three, The U.S. Interstate Highway System;
> four, The Kennedy Space Center;
> five, The Panama Canal;
> six, The Trans-Alaskan Pipeline;
> and seven is Hoover Dam."

It lofts up with the majesty of Beauty itself, and you marvel at what manner of men could have conceived the possibility of building such a wonder.

7. The Hoover Dam, 1935 (from *America the Beautiful: An Introduction to Our Seven Wonders*)

6

Perhaps the Book of Genesis is the first and most famous list of wonders. Today, however, such rosters of remarkable things are common in America.

Whenever I visit a city for the first time, I always notice the gold stars on storefronts—"Voted Best Barbershop," ". . . Mexican Food," ". . . Auto Repair." My brother, who prides himself on his ability to spot "quality trends," as he calls them, has sworn for years by *Boston Magazine's* annual "Best Of" issue.

He says that living by the list is like living in a perfect world. And the list has grown so comprehensive each year that, these days, my brother seldom has to live without perfection. He has found, for example, a "professional scalper" with the best last-minute Bruins ticket deals, a launderer known for having the best-pressed cuffs, and a sportsman's lodge with the best range for skeet shooting—a sport my brother has taken up simply out of awe of it being listed.

Another purveyor of perfection has gone so far as to publish a book-length list, entitled *The Best of Everything*, which includes the Best Sexy Animal (the female giraffe), the Best Labor-Saving Device (the guillotine), the Best Vending Machine (a mashed-potato dispenser in Nottingham, England), and the Best Souvenir (a shrunken head from Quito, Ecuador).

Not to be outdone, proponents of the worst things in the world have published *The Worst of Everything*. On this list can be found the Worst Nobel Peace Prize Recipient (Henry Kissinger), the Worst Item Ever Auctioned (Napoleon's dried penis), the Worst Poem Ever Written ("The Child" by Friedreich Hebbel), and the Worst Celebrity Endorsement for a Car (Hitler, for the Volkswagen Bug: "This streamlined four-seater is a mechanical marvel. It can be bought on an installment plan for six Reichsmarks a week—including insurance!")

Now Isaac's mother leans over our seats and shows us both another brochure.

"Just think how happy they all must have been," she says, unfolding an artist's rendition of the future across our laps. "I sure wish I lived back then. You know?"

1939. Queens, New York.

She, Isaac, and I have just paid our fifty cents, and before us—miles wide—are promenades, sculptures, buildings, and glittery things, all laid out in perfect grids. "So bright and lovely," she says, "it makes me want to close my eyes." Even the people around us shine, sweaty inside their wool suits and skirts. There are thousands of them, Isaac decides—just like the people who walk around EPCOT.

"You know," he says. "The kind who you can't really tell are real or not."

We buy frankfurters, a guidebook, little silver spoons at every exhibition. We are here because—even as far west as Nevada, even as far into the future as 1999—we have heard that this is the greatest fair ever orchestrated on earth.

We start with Isaac's mom's list: the Gardens on Parade, the Town of Tomorrow, the House of Jewels, the Plaza of Light, Democracity.

Then we visit Isaac's list: the Futurama, the Academy of Sports, the Court of Power, the Lagoon of Nations, the Dome of the Heinz Corp.

And by the time we visit my list we have stumbled smack into the middle of the fair, inches from its epicenter, squinting back up at those dazzling fair trademarks known in our guidebook as *Trylon* and *Perisphere*. The obelisk and the globe stand like silence behind the roaring and spurting of ten giant fountains.

The two of them are like fountains behind the silence of our gaze.

One of them is stretched so high it scrapes the color from the sky. The other is arched playfully on its own curved back.

The obelisk, we read, is 610 feet tall ("That's 50 feet taller than the Washington Monument!" our guidebook claims). The sphere is 180 feet in diameter ("The largest globe in the state of New York!").

Both objects are words that never before existed. And despite all the euphoria surrounding them in '39, all the family photos posed in front of them, the silverware and shaving kits and Bissell Carpet Sweepers that bore their images, *Trylon* and *Perisphere* never made it into our lexicon.

At the foot of them, I can't see why.

One is like a list, the other is like a wonder. But I don't say this aloud.

"An arrow and a bull's-eye!" one of us blurts out. And so they are. Perfectly.

Or one is like an ancient scroll unrolled; the other is an orb of indecipherable glyphs. One is how we describe a fantasy; the other is what we've secretly dreamt.

Shoulder to shoulder, we three look them up, then down. Our mouths hang wide—with *awe*—filled with them.

I remember the first list of wonders that I ever knew. One year, an old man on our street told my mother that he had once been a college professor, a master of Latin and Greek. Within days I was studying classics with him. I had just turned eight.

My tutor, Mr. Newcomb, lived alone among statuary and

plaster casts of temple friezes. Tapestries padded his walls. I met with him each day in the barest room of his house: a desk, two chairs, a lamp, a rug, and seven hanging woodcuts of the seven ancient wonders.

Some days, instead of reading, Mr. Newcomb beguiled me with trivia about the hanging wonders on his walls. And some days, strewn over the years, he divulged their secrets. Why, for instance, the curse of the Pyramids in fact is real; where, in Turkey, the Colossus' body parts are actually hidden; what, according to Vatican documents, which Mr. Newcomb alone had read in Rome, Napoleon "felt" as he pissed on the charred remains of Diana's great temple.

Later, Mr. Newcomb's woodcuts of the seven ancient wonders became mine once he had died. At that point, however, I had only managed to grasp the first conjugation in Latin, so for years after, until I could return to Latin in school, the ancient wonders lived beside me in a parallel present tense.

I have them still. They hang around—dark, worn—reminding me of the last wonderful secret my tutor left: that he had never studied Latin, never read the classics. That he had never traveled to Rome, nor much farther beyond our town.

He had never actually liked school.

Yet what he had was curiosity. Crustiness. An air of scholastic formality. He had a dustiness that was reliable. A home adorned tastefully, lessons always prepared for me, cookies, milk, stories that kept me rapt. He had a knack, which was his lure, for both the mundane and fantastic.

The black-breasted roadrunner, my favorite bird, is that
black-breasted roadrunner there.

The bird hurries past our bus, darting up the mountain pass as we slowly descend its peak. I am awakened by our driver's voice and my ears popping as we slide into the valley. Everyone else, everyone except for Isaac and the one-way man, is asleep. They chat across the center aisle.

"I'm gonna live there," says the one-way man, when Isaac asks what he'll do when we arrive at the dam.

"You can live there?" Isaac asks.

"Well, I'm gonna," says the man.

Isaac's mom, I know, would want me to intervene here, tell Isaac the man's just joking with him. Tell Isaac the one-way man is crazy.

But when Isaac starts talking about his computer game, and the one-way man explains how the concave wall of the Hoover Dam would be awesome for skateboarding, it is they who stop, mutually—nowhere conclusive and without any care.

They sit back in their seats, stare forward awhile, and fall asleep.

7

continents, days per week, Deadly Sins, Epochs of Man according to Shakespeare, hills of Rome, liberal arts, perfect shapes, planets in the Ptolemaic system, Pleiades in Greek myth, Sacraments, seas, Sleepers of Ephesus, wives of Bluebeard, wonders of Yemen, Years War

Door No. Two

The Wonders of the Bat World; The Wonders of the Beetle World; The Wonders of Blue Grass: As Seen Through Blue Glass with Fifteen Silhouette Illustrations Included; The Wonders of Bodily Strength and Skill in All Ages and Countries; The Wonders of Britain, and Where to Find Them.

The Wonders of California; Caribou; Cells; The Wonders of the Certainty of the World; The Circus: Man, Monkey, and Dog Wonders; The Wonders of the Colorado Desert: Its Rivers and Mountains, Its Canyons and Springs; The Wonders of the Creator and the Creature.

The Wonders of Dairy Cattle; Divine Love; Draft Horses; Dreams; Dunes; Dust; The Wonders of Dying.

Martha Graham,
Audio Description Of

audio description of,

As if a newsreel were spinning the unforgettable images of, as if by saying *red* and *walks across* and *downstage right,* sound could stand in for . . . I am standing in the mezzanine of an enormous old theatre, narrating into a microphone everything I see. I'm an audio describer, which means there are a dozen blind audience members listening right now to my voice, trusting me to report accurately all the physics of this dance—all the lighting, all the fabric, all the color, all the motion—all without the meaning. Which means I'm their eyes, the head usher reminds me, but not their interpreter. Which means words like *scary* and *boring* and *like* and *therefore* are out of the question. And the same goes for *which reminds me of,* though it's what I'm thinking, can't stop thinking of.

author's first encounter with,

Mother first brought me to see this dance, *Clytemnestra,* when I was nine. We were in Boston, at the brand-new Wang Center, and she meant for that night to be my introduction to

Art. We dressed up, had dinner downtown, were scheduled to meet the dancers after. But I got hot in my velour seat, my stiff wool suit, and it was dark in the theatre, and the lady in front of me smelled of lavender and liturgy, and halfway through I had to pee, and there weren't any words, anyway. So I don't remember much about the dance. All I can remember is a lady dressed in black slipping into her husband's red-draped bedchamber . . . Then I took my eyes off the stage for a second, and I think I'd have to blame all that blank space in the theatre for distracting me—the huge air between the stage and us—the dusk dangling above the audience, and above that: the midnight infinities of a ceiling seething with serenades of seraphs and their lyres, the ornate chandelier blooming more opulent in the dark, the hazard of a space in which the brink of reality and the outbreak of fantasy could, in a flash, collapse in each other's arms. It was that dark, a black-as-pitch lapse redolent of anything. So in that moment, when I looked away from the stage, when I glanced up into the air, I saw two statues from nooks on opposite sides of the theatre rendezvous in front of me. Midair, lodged in the penumbra between audience and stage. I watched Apollo, then Sappho. His breath drenched with innuendo, she wiping spit from her chin. And then, as if nothing had happened, I looked back to the stage and Agamemnon was dead, and Clytemnestra was spinning in that red cloth, and Apollo and Sappho were back in their nooks, looking as innocent as statues.

autobiography by,

The same year she died, Martha Graham published *Blood Memory*, a memoir. There's no beginning to it, really; no ending, intentionally. It is said that Martha wrote the book on her deathbed, dictating into a recorder whatever sprang to mind. Her words wander as you'd expect them to: dates, images, people from her life walk on and off the stage, out of order. I struggled to line them up one day, making little mounds of Martha here and there. It didn't work, though. There's no index.

business management of,

"In the Graham Company's centennial year, business managers signed with Danskin to turn some of Graham's early costume designs into retail streetwear. Danskin reproduced them, seam for seam, in black-stretch cotton jersey, knock-out, understated garb for a host of New York's best-dressed teens."

(Harper's Bazaar)

Campbell, Joseph, first encounter with,

Rumor has it that there were crab cakes, red punch, slaw. That he and she were young teachers at Bennington, and that one day, at a summer mixer in Vermont, Martha started talking about the Brontës and their fondness for pixies on the moor. He moved a little closer. Took a sip of punch. Martha, is it? You know, when you talk about fairy folk, you are really entering the world of the unconscious, and these creatures you say that come out of the fairy hills, well, they are manifestations of the psyche. What you are really doing is tapping into the unconscious memories of the human race. Then she said, Tell me.

colors worn by,

At first white, only white. White saris, white silk kimonos, white boleros, tank suits, scarves, foundations. It gave her the appearance of a small Oriental girl, someone said. And it never hid movement, which is why she insisted that her dancers wear it, too. But when Halston took over her costume designing in the 1960s, he didn't like the way the dancers were like dust mops on the stage—all that gunk from the floor clinging to his pristine vision of each dance. This was around the time when Martha stopped dancing. Soon her Company appeared all over the world in gold foil—a giant sparkle—so that movement under the blazing lights was preceded by a glint of glitter, a flash and flicker, and motion itself passed, anticlimactically, by.

drinking habits of,

So bad one year that she went into a coma.

epitaph, as if by,

"Was he ever anything other than dead, except the day he was killed?"

> (Clytemnestra on Agamemnon,
> *Oresteia*)

as expensive friend,

Imagine London, 1966, at Covent Garden. Opening night of the Company's European tour, and Martha is wearing a Halston, a gold scintillation. The performance is perfect and applause lasts "minutes," according to reports. The golden glow walks onstage. A microphone lowers from the flies. "I would never have had this great experience if it had not been for one man," she said. Her patron at the time was Robin Howard, a man who had been selling off his hotels, restaurants, and jewels for years in order to fund Martha and her Company. "If it were not for this man's help and support, I would not be here today," she said. For some reason, Martha had never before thanked Howard publicly for his patronage. So on that night, Howard rose happily to join Martha on the stage. "If it were not," she said, "for Halston," then flew off into the wings. At which point the spotlight must have caught the sequins of her gown at an awkward, glaring angle. He teared.

facial structure of,

Always. Looking through a pile of newspaper clippings, I keep thinking, *always*. Same broad smile, enormous teeth, long jaw, cheeks polished to an apex. Her eyes are dragged to the sides of her face along heavy ruts of eyeliner. It was always glamorous, in every photo for ninety-seven years. Halston ensured it. Dior before him. And after them, Donna Karan. Capezio designed tiny slippers for her. In the streets of New York, Martha was an ancient China doll. Too precious to touch the ground, she seemed to levitate between the two stars escorting her. Her head was held high—not her chin, but her head—so that in the *New York Post,* in *Vanity Fair,* in *People Magazine,* I don't notice her feet immediately, how clutching the arms of Madonna and Cher, Lila Wallace and Betty Ford, Liz Taylor and William Schuman, Martha floats like an angel already, like contempt for gravity.

father's influence on,

George Graham was a psychiatrist, a pioneer in the study of nervous disorders. He watched rats, monkeys, lions, elephants, he watched his patients' gestures. He watched his daughters, too. He said, "Movement never lies." When she was sixteen, Martha wanted to see Ruth St. Denis dance in Los Angeles. He took her. Together the two watched St. Denis "perform karma," as she called it. After Martha's father died, she tried to learn how to dance. She told herself, "Movement never lies." She moved to New York and joined the Greenwich Village Follies. At that time dance was vaudeville, minstrel, Broadway, ballroom. Serious dance was European ballet. St. Denis's dance was idealized Greek. But Martha's dance was scary, primal, Jung, and Freud. She told the small group of teenage girls who had answered her ad for dancers that *from the pelvis sharp, from the pelvis lotus lotus lotus sharp when the great overwhelming unconscious tide, the great unconscious lotus sharp.* And by the end of her speech the girls were in positions unnatural, bloody, raw. "A contraction. A Martha Graham contraction," Bette Davis once called it, remembering the night Graham taught her how to cry. The girls held their cramping guts high as lances in the air. And then Graham suddenly stopped the audition. And maybe then there was silence after. Sobbing hushed in the far corners of the room. Heavy breathing here and there. Maybe a girl ran out of the room, her hands clutched around her ears. What did Martha say that afternoon? After everything, what did she bother saying? She gathered up the lotus petals, stacked the spears against the wall. Martha looked around and thought, Enough. Movement proved enough.

Hawkins, Eric, marriage to,

Did you see him on PBS last night? Sitting there, same short haircut, same hard build after eighty-five years—though it's hard to believe Martha once called him "The Torso"—he said things like *pipsqueak;* like, *the prophetic thing about the place of my birth;* like, *I was her whipping boy,* and I just wanted to scream. I mean, he went to Harvard to study Greek; Martha hardly finished high school. And yet he waltzed into her Company—the first guy to join them, the first trained in ballet—and said, off the cuff, that maybe the Greek tragedies would be "interesting" to explore, and he didn't think she'd take him seriously? He didn't think she'd go to town with that? What was he thinking when he sat there last night, knowing that the woman is dead, knowing full well that the world has been waiting to hear him talk about their breakup for the first time, anywhere, in forty years? He said things like *indulge,* like *her private emotional storms,* like, "The use of art to show psychology was something I wanted to avoid. I think if she had just gone on the way she had done in some of her earlier works, now they . . . *they* were life-giving and . . . and they were glorious. What I don't think Martha ever understood is that I was just trying my darndest to protect the old girl."

loneliness as strength to,
    see as attracted to homosexuals,
    see ego of,
    see indifference and carelessness in,
    see nighttime creativity of,
    see as vessel of higher force,

the many uses for a prop in the hands of,
    Woman in black (Clytemnestra) enters empty stage from right flanked by two attendants who carry red cloth. Clytemnestra moves stage left & sits on throne. Man dressed in gold (Agamemnon) enters from stage right on litter. Clytemnestra approaches Agamemnon upstage center. Agamemnon steps off litter, bows to Clytemnestra, circles with spear in hand three times. Returns to litter. Woman with long hair & holding staff (Cassandra) enters quickly from stage right. Clytemnestra's attendants spread red cloth on ground. Clytemnestra kneels at foot of Agamemnon's litter & extends hand. Agamemnon extends foot & steps off litter. Clytemnestra pulls hand away. Agamemnon stumbles off litter. Circles in place three times. Pulls Clytemnestra up from ground. She turns away, he pulls her back, lifts her into air. Agamemnon carries

Clytemnestra downstage to red cloth on floor. Lays her down on it, lies down on her. She wriggles underneath him, he wriggles on top. Agamemnon rises, steps over Clytemnestra, moves to Cassandra stage right & kneels. Clasps waist. Agamemnon rises & moves upstage, spear in hand, stands on litter. Clytemnestra rises from red cloth downstage & moves stage left toward throne. Attendants carry red cloth upstage & drape over Agamemnon's litter. Cassandra moves upstage center to litter. Lies with Agamemnon behind red cloth. Clytemnestra removes sword from behind gold throne. Enters red cloth draped over litter. Lights lower. Red lights rise. Drape opens to reveal Clytemnestra puncturing Agamemnon with sword. Drape closes. Lights lower. Red lights rise. Drape opens & reveals Clytemnestra puncturing Cassandra with sword. Attendants remove red cloth from litter & spread downstage on ground. Clytemnestra kneels before it. Lies down on it. Rolls. Kneels. Rises slowly as red cloth cloaks her, surrounds her, coils around as she spins in place, faster, & faster, & faster. Lights dim.

mink coat advertisement of,
  "Tacky."

(The New York Times)

Mycenae and,
  Clytemnestra's in Hades. This is after her husband sacrificed their daughter. This is after the war, when he returned

— 33 —

from Troy. When Clytemnestra and her lover slew her husband and his lover, then tried to get on with their lives. And tried to ignore the ghosts of Mycenae. I could tell you about Mycenae. It's a haunted place. There is more than just the Lion Gate. There are Circle Graves you could lose yourself in, walls that spin ancestry into myth. Or, as she would say: into blood memory. The way our memories seep even from myth. I was ten when I first went there, and too young to have forgotten her spinning dance, but too young to have understood what myth she was unraveling and revealing in brick and grit and spit. Mother and I got lost among those ruins once. But please bear in mind that it was dark. She brought me there weeks after leaving my father, so it was secretive, of course. It was still not right in those days for the woman to leave the man, so the air was red, you see. It was reddening, when we left, in that early cloak of sky.

parenthetical performances by,

When she wrote in *The Notebooks* under the chapter heading "Preliminary Studies for Clytemnestra," that "walls, if they had mouths, might tell tales all too plainly," what she meant (paraphrasing Homer there), what she meant (nodding to the expression of *flies on a wall*) (to the night King Belshazzar saw on his wall), what she meant (alongside it quoting Woolf, who quoted Joyce, remembering the story of . . .), what she meant (figuring: only she would read these notes); (figuring, and lingering, and letting the long thoughts through); when she wrote in her wispy, bubbled script, in her high-looping *L,* in pursuit of swiftly fading images from her noontime naps *(What if the stage were raked? . . . If no dancer spent more than one dollar on each costume? . . . What if we stood still instead? . . . If only Orpheus had said? . . . What of the forest to the world, of the conscience to unconsciousness?),* like a net poised above words, she . . .; when she wrote *(ancestral footprints push a dancer, so that you get to the point where your body is something else)* all through the night *(I want to go to the top and I don't want to take anybody with me),* what she meant *(These walls),* what she meant—do you follow?—what she meant *(I am a thief and I am not ashamed; I steal from Plato, Picasso . . .),* what she meant, by taking the bull by the horns, by wearing her heart on her sleeve, by putting her cart before the horse, and sowing her wild oats, is that these motions have matter also, these lines have in-betweens, these lights have shadows, these walls have mouths.

photographs of,

My favorite photograph of Martha is the one of her rehearsing the spinning scene in *Clytemnestra.* She's looking at me in the photograph, but the rest of her body has begun to turn away. She's midspin, in the photograph. She's nowhere near figuring out her character yet. Nothing, in that photograph, has happened yet. She isn't a ghost. She isn't a killer. Not a mistress. Not betrayed. She has not yet read Homer, not yet Aeschylus, not yet started wondering how she got trapped in this fight between the domestic and heroic. Not yet clenched her teeth against Athena's smoothing-over of history. Not yet put her foot down. Not yet moved the other back. Not yet started spinning, nor yet so fast, so blurred, so emphatically that things both swirled away and toward her, centrifugally, like a sparkle, like a thousand filaments hurtling into space, like a star unraveling herself to dust. Not yet. Not yet. In the photograph Martha has not yet discovered the red cloth she will use in performance, so in rehearsal she uses a net.

psychoanalysis sought by,
　　Never. Instead, in a heap of letters ranging over twenty years, Martha corresponded with Frances Wickes, the lay analyst and writer, who had also been Jung's mistress.

quotation pertinent to,
　　"I have learned by experience that the dead do not lie still."
　　　　　　　　　　　　　　(Clytemnestra, in Marguerite Your-
　　　　　　　　　　　　　　cenar's *Fires*)

some of you are listening only and care not about the meaning of,
　　It must have something to do with those names the terms and titles the dance words for Bourre Treading Knee Vibration March-Jump March-Jump Javanese her tendency to swoon at Knee-Crawl swish of thighs in tights Dart Dart across the stage like Lunge and titles saying Punch and the Judy saying Maple Leaf Rag saying A Study in Lacquer Errand into the Maze Every Soul is a Circus Four Insincerities Four Casual Developments From a XII-Century Tapestry

Alcetis Phaedra One More Gaudy Night it is just the sound isn't it of her eyesight going so bad she once addressed a scarf left on a chair by one of the dancers saying You needn't wait any longer Mary I don't think we'll get to your part until later.

spinning sensation caused by,

I don't know if you've got it too, but I have this feeling I can't explain. As if I'm being given more than I need to know. As if "more than" is not enough. It makes audio description difficult, to say the least. And at times I get so angry I wish I could make it all just stop and stand there, as stiffly, as surely, as statues stand.

unavailable footage of,

Afterward, Mother drove us home, talking to the rearview mirror. I think, "A dance part window, part glass," is what she called it. But what I was thinking as she said this was how huge and black the theatre felt with all that space unfilled. For months after, I tried figuring out the plot of the dance, linking scenes together across broad swaths of boredom and dream and blank. *Why? Why was she in hell? Why was he so late? Why was she wearing red? And how'd it rub off on him? Was she spinning, or was she reeling? Was that happy, or sad?* Years after, I finally called the Graham Company to borrow a video of that dance, but the woman on the screen wasn't Martha anymore. Black bunned hair, black triangular eyes, the substitute dancer was made up to look like Martha playing Clytemnestra. A role now part mythic, part Martha. I'm still searching for a version of her spin that hasn't yet been tucked into history. Inside that interval is the crack that's left after a culture is crushed, before another is forged; a yellow bruise, a broken arm, ranks of soldiers splayed like scabs across the landscape. There are the dark evenings alone, in waiting, the long preparation for revenge. There are broken dishes, photo albums burning in the sink, a lamp smashed against the wall. In the morning, we left so fast that my mother slammed the door on my father's arms. But one hand, through a crack in the window's glass, hung for a moment, dripping, as we drove away.

voice of,

Outside Naples, in ancient Cumae, there is a cave approached by a five-hundred-foot tunnel. Locals say it is the sibyl's cave, constructed by a Greek tyrant in the sixth century B.C. The sibyl, like all Greek oracles, never answered a question directly. Around the subject, through it, an amalgam of, her voice was like the gurgled sound of waves that fills the tunnel, as if a conch were pressed to the opening of that ear along the shore. In the Golden Age of Radio, waves were what we listened to, while at the same time, in Greenwich Village, Martha was making soundless art—something obscured from the masses by the silence of its message. So even though her friends thought that she was crazy, when the March of Dimes approached her with an offer to do a radio show, Martha grabbed it—becoming "Miss Hush": a voice that broadcast weekly from her dance studio, a mystery millions tuned in to hear, a game show in which Miss Hush provided clues as to her true identity, week after week, until, months into her new stardom, Martha Graham announced the winner—a woman from St. Louis—although Martha's old friends in the Village knew who the real winner was. Decades later, when she left the hospital after her last bout with cirrhosis, Martha vowed to make some changes. It was the early 1980s, and she was no longer avant-garde. To save herself, she incorporated. In 1984, in the Graham Company's new school brochure, Martha's name appears seven times in the first nine lines, and after it, each time—small as a linger, or a last gasp—a little TM appears, as it does on the Martha Graham Coffee Mugs™, Sweatshirts™, Tote Bags™. At her most famous, the sibyl was visited by emperors, by warriors, by even gods. Legend has it that when Apollo stopped by one day to visit the sibyl, he was so struck by the oracle that he offered her one wish come true. She asked for immortality. And he granted it. But not long into her eternal life, the sibyl discovered the fatality of her request: she had forgotten to ask for eternal youth as well. The last account we have of the sibyl comes from Rome. Tourists in the fourth century A.D. say that in the dilapidated Temple of Apollo there was a tiny jar labeled *Sibylla* from which there trickled a voice, a sound so small it was vapor.

water feared by,

In December 1941, the Company sailed to Cuba for a week of performances. Martha, terrified that the ship would sink, that she would have to swim, that she would drown, took something that made her sleepy. Maybe she dreamt of the antediluvian. When the land was parched, harmless, easy to read. Before all this water under the bridge. Before this: the detritus, the flotsam and jetsam churned up onstage, the drinkable, the unquenchable, the can't-put-a-stop-to. In her mind the waters soon flooded her dream, billowed and shirred, and slowly, as if a whirlpool from a cave, as if blood were swept out from under the rug, as if it clung to her like a cloak, she rose up and turned, she heaved the waters upon her shoulders, the waters and all their lore, off of the sea's rocky

what she does,	*what she heaves,*
stage floor.	shore.

Door No. Three

The Wonders of the East: Vol. 3; The Wonders of Egrets, Bitterns and Herons; The Wonders of Egypt; The Wonders of Electricity; The Wonders of Elephants; The Wonders of Elora: Or, the Narrative of a Journey to the Temples and Dwellings Excavated Out of a Mountain of Granite and Extending Upwards of a Mile and a Quarter at Elora, in the East Indies, by the Route of Poona, Ahmed-Nuggur, and Toka, Returning by Dowlutabad and Aurungabad, with Some General Observations on the People and Place.

The Wonders of Fatima; The Wonders of Fire and Water: Or, Talks with Children About God's Power, Love and Wisdom, as Seen in Fire and Water; Flightless Birds; The Wonders of Florida Flowers; The Wonders of Fossils; The Wonders of Foxes; The Wonders of Free-Grace: Or, a Compleat History of All the Remarkable Penitents That Have Been Executed at Tyburn and Elsewhere for These Last Thirty Years, to Which is Added a Sermon Preached in the Hearing of a Condemn'd Malefactor Immediately Before His Execution.

Flat Earth Map: An Essay

I. Legend

"A legend is a symbolization of information in a map; it gives, in abbreviated form, most of the facts that are needed to decode a map and enable its readers to plot trips into heretofore unknown terrains."[1]

> (Dr. Paul A. Riffel, *Reading Maps: An Introduction,* Chicago: Hubbard Press, 1979)

II. Coordinates

"E-13"

"Page 16, Lancaster"

"This place is flat."

---

[1]For example, *Once upon a time the world climbed up a tall tree toward heaven, but when their god looked down and howled at them, then the world turned red as fruit leaves and then fell,* could be read as a legend.

"Here, five minutes from town, ranger-led tours explore a healthy Joshua Tree woodland. Each spring the desert floor is covered with fiddleneck, flowering beavertail, desert dandelion, desert aster, desert poppies, and sand verbena. The pronghorn have disappeared, but tortoises still munch on flowers near their burrows."

"Piped water, picnic tables, stoves, flush toilets, and sanitary dump stations are available nearby. Wheelchair accessible, too."

"Specialties include prime rib, steak, chicken, and seafood, trout, catfish, and other local varieties."

"Green marble in lobby."

"Ice. HBO."

"Welcome, Old Chateau Abbey, World Headquarters, International Flat Earth Zetic Society, California, USA, Earth."

(U.S. Mail Stop, 18311 East Avenue
J, Lancaster, California 93539)

"Welcome," Charles Johnson says.[2]

"Welcome."[3]

---

[2]Meet 10:30. Leave 7:00. Get gas. Hwy 5 (right on Vine, look for signs), Fwy 14 east. Go 90+ mi NE (past Angeles National Forest, Ed AF Base), take Ave J exit (Jack in Box end of ramp), then right, keep going, through town, go 19 mi—past Deli Video halfway, then two ranches after—when past Blvd 15 start looking, 18311 East Ave J, "When you see garbage all over the highway, that's me. Take that

right. Keep going, then keep going," past pages, past chunks of books, then past single leaves of newsletters trailing on the gusts of cars—and, closer, through gate—a floorlamp, still shaded, will be standing upright in the desert, white china sediment settling into sandstone—and, closer—an easy chair in recline, a bamboo bird cage crushed, a china closet bare, an armoire on its side, underwear, cans of food, a mirror blinking wildly—there: glimpse of door hinge; there: piece of sky; there: serif?; filigree?; cornflower bloom on kitchen teacups; here: "begot Kenan, begot Jared, begot Enoch, begot Lamech"; here: sage growth, charcoal, penny; here: zipper; here: foot track; here: colander; here: ashtray; spatula; terra-cotta-roof-piping piece; here: bird-flying-by, and hoofprint, and once there were horses here; and license plate, and window frame, and windowpane . . . and: sun glare; bottle cap; sailor's-button-fused-to-lightbulb screw; keyhole; fire tong; *Stockholm, Finland, Leningrad;* curdled-scented-candle pond; here: spoon; here: something scuttled by and I jumped without looking; here: switchplate; heel tip; fifty cents; here: axe edge; here: BEST IF USED BY; here: three-ring binder; here: silver-underneath-of-copper-pot lid; watchband, hook and clasp; hubcap, Mercury; phone cord, coiled; crack-in-beam; here: black-iron-scratch-in-plant-stand grid; here: nail-in-wood; here: blue pills; here: earring post; here: he: is.

---

[3]You must imagine him saying this from the doorway of his trailer parked some yards away from the wreckage of his house, still musty and charred eight months after the fire. Imagine, too, Mr. Johnson waving. He is eighty-three. White hair, white beard. Cigar in his mouth. White V-neck T-shirt, little yellow beneath the arms, not tucked into pajama bottoms, and, for what it's worth, slippers. There are dogs in and out of the door. There is a generator clanging nearby.

III. Longitude

LANCASTER, Calif. (AP) Fire destroyed the home of the president of the Flat Earth Society and burned membership rosters for this international organization of contrarians.

"It's all gone," said Charles Johnson. His lonely house near Saddleback Butte State Park doubled as world headquarters of the society, whose 3,500 members reject science and satellite photos.

"I hope people will write to us wondering what happened so we'll be able to get their names again. Right now, we're really at a loss," said Johnson on Thursday.

Authorities weren't sure what started the fire. Johnson said he was watching television when he noticed flames on the front porch. He made an emergency call, then helped his wife, Marjory, who cannot walk and uses an oxygen tank to breathe. The couple lived in the house since 1972, the same year Johnson became president of the society on the death of Samuel Shenton of Britain.

"My wife has been sick, and I've been busy with her," he said. "It's hard keeping up with my presidential duties, but I'm not giving up. We'll get our members back."

The couple has moved into a trailer house on their property, shaken but still convinced that round-earthers are being taken for a ride.

(September 29, 1995, Associated Press Wire)

Marjory Waugh Johnson, 78, of emphysema, at her home in Lancaster, Saturday.

(May 1996, *Desert Mailer News*)

IV. Latitude[4]

"I advise all my readers who have become Zetetic not to be content with anything less than Justice; and also not to look with disfavour upon the objections of their opponents. Should such objections be well or even plausibly fended, they will only tend to free us from error, and to purify and exalt our Zetetic philosophy. In a word, let us make friends, or, at least, be friendly and useful instruments of our enemies; and, if we cannot convert them to the better cause, let us carefully examine their objections, fairly meet them if possible, and always make use of them as beacons for our future guidance."

(Samuel Rowbotham, "A Preface," *Earth Not a Globe: An Experimental Inquiry into the True Figure of the Earth, Proving It a Plane, Without Orbital of Axial Motion, and the Only Known Material World; Its True Position in the Universe, Comparatively Recent Formation, Present Chemical Condition and Approaching Destruction by Fire,* &c., &c., &c., London: Day Books, 1873)

---

[4] Charles Johnson _____, which is not common knowledge in Lancaster, California, and so it is not something one would learn upon immediately arriving in town for an interview with the man. Neither would one learn this by visiting his local market, Joe's—"Quiet guy, in once a month"—nor the Copy King who

"We do not want members who are stupid, mindless, brute beasts with two feet only aim to scoff our work. People of goodwill who seek truth also known as FACTS Welcome! Our Society of Zetetics have existed for at least 6,000 years, extent of recorded history. Extensive writing from A.D. 1492. We have been and are the Few, the Elite, the Elect, use Logic Reason are Rational. Summed up, we are Sane and or have Common Sense as contrasted to the 'herd' who are unthinking and uncaring. We have absorbed the Universal Zetetic Society of Great Britain, the work of Samuel Rowbotham

---

prints his newsletters—"Long as he pays"—nor Marjory's grave— "she loved the furried/fairfeathered/all God's creatures"—nor even by heading twenty minutes from town toward his house, turning into his driveway, through the refuse of his ranch, greeting him from the car door some yards away from the trailer, where he stands, waving, and toward whom you walk, your hand out to catch his two large soft ones, which fall, it seems, off his body, onto yours; nor, even, once he leads you inside, offers tea from a pan; nor as you sit on the two sheetless mattresses in the living/sleeping/eating room of his house and take out the recorder; nor once his telling starts; nor once your looking starts, lifting and fingering and piercing the dark smoky air, over and over again, to nothing, no end . . . ; not even then would you know this. Alone in this trailer—even alone for some time as he goes out to pee and you sit among his Bible flat open, the Fotomat envelopes, writing pad closed—would you know what to look for? what does it look like? why is it? Outside, an old man, alone, in the desert, funnels with his hands a long strand of sighs into the earth, and they pool around him, and he cries.

1888, Wilber Glen Voliva 1942, Samuel Shenton 1971. Zetetic: from Zeto, to seek and search out; Prove, as contrasted to theoretic, which means to guess, to hope, to suppose, but NOT to 'prove.' Science 'proves' earth a 'ball' by 'scripture' words, we PROVE earth FLAT by experiment, demonstrated and demonstrable. Earth Flat is Fact."

(Charles Johnson, *Omni Magazine*,
1978, advertisement)

V. DEGREES

CJ: So you've come to the flat earth[5]

I: (recorder static)

CJ: This is it you're in it

I: Let me thank you first off for agreeing to meet with me
  . sir

CJ: The whole world depends on you

------

[5]When Charles Johnson says *flat earth,* he means a disk of floating land masses resembling the seven continents with a suspension of water encircling them. But floating on what? suspended from what? This we do not know, about which Johnson is clear. He is similarly frank on the issue of polar regions: North is central; South peripheral, outlining whatever form the flat world comprises. Beyond the South Pole is neither space nor void, neither secret nor imaginable. Beyond the South Pole is merely *beyond,* a boundary undiscovered and nonexistent and therefore *impossible to sail off the edge of,* Johnson says. I wish I could follow this. Mr. Johnson gave me a map of

I: Well

CJ: It really does

I: It means a lot to me

CJ: The world is in one hell of a shape I'll tell you

I: How exactly do you

CJ: In respects of physically it's in halfway decent shape

I:

CJ: But the thinking process is so far gone it's almost impossible to retrieve anything

I: Would you say because of the school systems or

CJ: Because of the general system the thing we're battling is the complete ignorance of the human being and the fact that he is you know a ring-tailed monkey

I: Right

CJ: And the poor soul don't even realize it

I: Right

---

his earth when I visited him in Lancaster recently. I had it matted and framed and hung it over the couch in my apartment in Boston, and now when my friends come to visit they stare—from the dining room, through the den, to the wall above the couch, at the acreage of shore and ocean and what's called "southern ice." My guests cast their eyes deeply into the map: into the faint regions of Latin letters on the land forms, which are centuries faint; into the black waves that indicate *wave* in "South Ocean Seas"; into the smudge on the map, up there in the corner; into the white margins of the earth.

CJ: And he wants to fight it and he'll pull out his six-shooter and shoot you down in a minute

I: Right

CJ: If you want to argue with him about it

I: Right

CJ: And still he'll tell you this world is going round and round and round and round and not only that it's spinning around at a hundredthousandblahblahblah and oh we could go on endlessly besides that Jesus went up I say well where's up?

VI. PROJECTIONS

"A map projection is what cartographers call the system by which the round surface of the earth is transformed in order to display it on a flat surface."[6]

(J.S. Keates, *Understanding Maps,*
London: Longman Press, 1982)

---

[6]Charles Johnson has made many predictions. He predicted, for example, that shortly after his arrival in the Lancaster desert fifteen years ago the city would be named official Flat Earth Territory by the United States in an effort to placate the growing number of Society members in the voting population. Today, with 107,000 residents, Lancaster is at the hub of the space shuttle industry, sendng nearly a third of its population daily to Edwards Air Force Base for shuttle construction, repairs, and support services. The sky,

"Now, if the Earth is a globe, and is 25,000 English statute miles in circumference, the surface of all standing water must have a certain degree of convexity: every part must be an arc of a circle. From the summit of any such arc there will exist a curvature or declination of 8 inches in the first statute mile; in the second mile the fall will be 32 inches; and so on. Therefore:

The curvature in 1 statute mile will be 8 inches.

"	"	" 2	"	miles	"	" 32	"	.
"	"	" 3	"	"	"	" 6	feet.	
"	"	" 4	"	"	"	" 10	"	.
"	"	" 5	"	"	"	" 16	"	.
"	"	" 10	"	"	"	" 266	"	.
"	"	" 20	"	"	"	" 600	"	.
"	"	" 30	"	"	"	" 1,066	"	.

. . .

The curvature in 25,000 statute miles will be 62,083,333 feet."

(Rowbotham, "Experiments Demonstrating the True Form of Standing Water, and Proving the Earth To Be a Plane")

----

streaked with jets, rotates and knots above Mr. Johnson's head. To dream anything in the desert is risky. Once, prophets like Buddha, Moses, even Brigham Young, found few challenges to their ideas in the desert: *tabula rasa,* far as the eye could see. Today, however, scan the horizon in Lancaster, California, and glean how to fit Mr. Johnson into this world—bunkers, runways, towers, and projectiles, mounting, arcing, whipping clouds overhead.

"If the Earth were a globe there certainly would be . . . if we could imagine the thing . . . 'anti-podes': 'people who' says dictionary 'live exactly on opposite side of the globe to ourselves have their feet opposite to ours . . . people who are HANGING DOWN HEAD DOWNWARDS! as we fancy to be head up, therefore our friends whom we have left behind head downwards proves the WHOLE THING A MYTH . . . A DREAM DELUSION snare . . . and instead no evidence at all to substantiate pop theory . . . hard proof Earth not Globe."

(Charles Johnson, "100 Proofs
Earth Not a Globe #14")

VII. Elevations

"An object which moves in an arc of a circle and returns to a given point in a given time, as the sun does to the meridian, must, of necessity, have completed a circular path in the twenty-four hours which constitute a solar day. To place the matter beyond doubt, the observations of arctic navigators may be referred to. Captain Parry and several of his officers, on ascending high land near the arctic circle, repeatedly saw, for twenty-four hours together, the sun describing a circle upon the southern horizon. Captain Parry writes:

'Very few of us had ever seen the sun at midnight; and this night, happening to be particularly clear, his broad red disk, curiously distorted by refraction and seeping majestically along the northern horizon, was an object of imposing grandeur which rivetted to the deck some of our crew who would perhaps have beheld with indifference the less imposing effect of the icebergs. The rays were too oblique to illuminate more than the irregularities of the floes, and falling thus partially on the grotesque shapes either really assumed by the ice or distorted by the unequal refraction of the atmosphere, so betrayed the imagination that it required no great exertion of fancy to trace, in various directions, architectural edifices, grottoes, and caves, here and there, glittering as if with precious metals.'"

(Rowbotham, "The True Distance of the Sun and Its Motion, Concentric with the Polar Centre")

"How about the space program in America and USSR? you ask? doesn't it prove earth globe 'sphere'? Quite simple, main thing to get is some 'proof' earth is ball-planet, but as I've said, no proof CAN BE FOUND FOR THE DELUSIONS OF LUNATICS globe world! Nick Kruchief in USSR in league with England started 'spook-nick' peep peep. HOAX! remember that? Purpose to 'prove' world ball and finally do away with GOD, bring the Russian people into total subjugation, no hope at all. As soon as spook-nick done, Vast campaign began to force atheism on the people, saying 'we have now proved world a tiny speck globe, world' SO CAN BE NO GOD ..."

(Johnson '85)

". . . The whole thing so false and fact is criminal-pervert fiends at JORDEL bank were really conducting it. Hee Haw, well, Nicks crime partner President Kennedy in USA, said . . . hey hey, the peons want to believe in spook-nick, beep beep, we'll pretend to go to the moon. We'll put entire goodwill of USA into it. At that time USA loved and trusted by the world . . ."

(Johnson '87)

". . . Also he told his henchmen . . . no worry boys, they'll be PLENTY OF JOBS, he was with the same gang of subversives CLANTON and his gang has. Well, somebody rubbed him out in Dallas, and of course all the decent people in government, all the ARMY NAVY MARINES knew ball was hoax . . ."

(Johnson '90)

". . . We were the only people who stayed honest and true and like the Disciples of Jesus and the Old Texas Rangers we found what was right and fell on the riot of madness, the delusions of idiots and disproved their screw-ballism, totally proved it flat . . ."

(Johnson '91)

". . . and NOTHING NOBODY can do about it."[7]

(Charles Johnson, 1993)

---

[7] I hold my bowl of tea while Mr. Johnson swigs a vitamin elixir. He has had pneumonia for some weeks now, but he recently checked himself out of a hospital when the doctors told him he had double pneumonia. *That,* he said, *is going too far.*

VIII. Scale

"For example, in order to depict great distances on a relatively small sheet of paper, maps must compress the actual size of the earth to the so-called map scale, itself an abstraction of reality because it has no counterpart in nature."[8]

(Arthur Robinson, *Choosing a World Map*, Washington, D.C.: American Surveying Corporation, 1988)

"Let A, B, R be a section of the earth's shadow at the distance of the moon; S, *n*, the path described by its centre, S, on the ecliptic; M, *n*, the relative orbit of the moon; M, *n*, S, *n*, being considered straight lines. Draw S, *o*, perpendicular to S, *n*, and S, *n*, to M, *n*; then *o*, and *n*, are in the places, with

---

[8]What if the world ignores him? What if it rolls away? In his trailer, Charles Johnson won't stop talking. I can't ask anything, I can't keep up. I change the tape for the third time, there is a chance the world's deflating. I say, hold on, let me ask a question, got to do my job. He says, cigar smoke in my eyes. Stands up to find a verse in Matthew. The clattering of a can outside. The dog's gnarl on a stuffed dog. So it's about perception, right, our culture per se, and not just the geography of the planet (I slip this in between the pages he's flipping through to find something else in)? What I want to ask him is what happens when we go unnoticed. Your line of questioning flames on the porch one night, he says. What happens when we go unnoticed? Something I write down writhes along the lines of paper in my notebook as it curls around my hand. It is blinding. What happens when the world goes flat for a moment, unnoticed?

respect to S, of the moon in opposition, and at the middle of the eclipse.

Let a = S, B = $h + p - q$, the radius of the section of the shadow.

Let f = the relative horary motion in longitude of the moon in the relative orbit, M, n.

Let l = S, o, the moon's latitude in opposition.

Let h = the moon's horary motion in the relative orbit.

Let g = the moon's horary motion in latitude.

Let w = the moon's semi-diametre."

(Rowbotham)

"Let there be light.

Let there be a vault between the waters to separate the water from water.

Let the waters under heaven be gathered into one place so the dry land may appear.

Let the earth produce fresh growth, let there be on the earth plants bearing seeds, fruit trees bearing fruit, each with seeds according to its kind.

Let there be lights in the heavens to separate the day from night, and let them serve as signs both for festivals and for seasons. Let them shine in the vault of heaven and let them give light on earth.

Let the waters teem with countless creatures, and let birds fly above earth across the vault of heaven.

Let the earth bring forth living creatures, according to their kind: cattle, reptiles, wild animals, all according to their kind.

Let us make man in our image and likeness to rule the fish in the sea, the birds of heaven, the cattle, all wild animals on earth, and the reptiles that crawl upon the ground."[9]

(God, *Old Testament*)

IX. Projections, ii

"When we consider that the surface of the earth is a vast structure of metallic oxides, sulphurets, and chlorides, intermingled with strata of compounds of carbon and hydrogen, and that, as we have already shown, a great portion of the lower parts of the earth is in a molten incandescent state, the earth itself an extended plane resting in and upon the waters of the great deep, fitly comparable to a large vessel or ship floating at anchor with its hold or lower compartments be-

---

[9]One of the earliest stories among human beings goes like this: Charles Johnson is born in the desert and stays there till he dies. Such simplicity, it should follow, would simplify a man. But it is cold, and the night with stones casts a net as broad as sky upon him. Soon the shivering Charles finds himself looking at knots in this patchwork and he wonders: what is it that these archers and these men with dogs and these large golden swans want from me? Every night they approach like an army and just stare. This is the night Charles finds himself screaming; staring back at the knots, and screaming; naming each one of them, and screaming more. He goes on screaming, staring, and naming until the dawn finally arrives, which is when Charles discovers that he can once again see clearly. He sees nothing, of course, yet he can see.

neath the water-line filled with burning materials, our knowledge of the nature of fire does not enable us to understand in what way the combustion can be prevented from extending when these burning materials increase and extend themselves, gradually creeping upwards toward the thousands of miles of veins filled with carbonaceous fuel, making impossible, unless the course of nature is arrested by some special interference, for the earth to remain in its present concrete condition. This much is clear."[10]

(Rowbotham, "Shall the Earth Be Destroyed by Fire?")

---

[10]I've never watched Charles Johnson in the process of writing one of his essays and, under the present circumstances, in light of his preceding hardships, and due to the imminent causes for alarm, it may be true that I never get to, that he never publishes *The Flat Earth News* again. Where will we be then?[a]

---

[a] There is, no doubt, a gap between what I am thinking at this moment and the moment that you are thinking of. Between me, writer, and you, reader, and the brink across which *knowledge* and *we* stare. But you know all this. Know that the spot which we essay together is seldom marked with an X. And yet we are always mapping the invisible, the unattainable, the erasable, the future or the past, the whatever-is-not-here—to ever futile ends. And yet, and yet his bold face. And yet his caps. Yet italics. Ellipses. Dash.

X. Magnetic Forces

"The talented lecturer Samuel Rowbotham is again in Greenwich, rivetting the attention of his audiences with an explanation of his experiments handled in a plain and easy manner. We say *submit,* because it seems impossible for anyone to battle with him, so powerful are the weapons he uses. Mathematicians argue with him at the conclusion of his lectures, but it would seem as though they held their weapons by the blade and fought with the handle, for sure enough they put the handle straight into the lecturer's hand."

(*Greenwich Free Press,* May 1862)

XI. Minutes

I: I'm wondering what keeps you going probably if I were in your shoes and the press contacted me to give interviews and all the articles ended up being cruel I would just pack up and say okay I believe what I believe

CJ: Sure

I: And so you know forget you

CJ: Well I'm the last of the knights

I: Hmm

CJ: I've got my white horse

I:

CJ: And I've ridden him all my life

I:

CJ: That's the only answer that's why I keep riding

I:

CJ: Until I die

I:

CJ: Maybe I'll never die[11]

I:

CJ: People say

---

[11]Suppose Charles Johnson believes that if he dies the greatest secret on earth will die with him. For me, this is what makes reading *The Flat Earth News* so breathtaking: he exhausts me. His breathlessness exhausts, and mocks, and bamboozles my logic, and therefore my life, and therefore I'm left, purely, with wonder. This is how not to die. Mr. Johnson outwits death with a prose peculiar to prophets, polemicists, pilgrims . . . only not to poets, for the silence after a line in a poem is like a little death, the way I imagine for him a complete poem would be like a suicide raid into the space he is struggling to fill. So I would think that at this point Mr. Johnson would be writing nonstop—lengthwise across the page, scrolls if he had them, around and around the walls of his trailer—. But, when I visited him, what struck me instead was a poem I noticed scratched into his Bible:

> This Flat Earth.
> Is the only known
> world in existence.
> Moses, all the Prophets,
> Jesus Christ, all affirm
> Earth center of Universe,

I:

CJ:

I:

CJ: Excuse me I get so

I: Sorry do you want to

CJ: No

I:

CJ: No no sentiment catches me and when it does I can't
help it

I: Of course

CJ: I can't help it this is why I just kept on with Marjory
with her twenty-four hours a day I stayed up all night
and all day trying to keep her alive why does a knight
go out and fight the dragon well he just does because

Flat and does not whirl around Sun.
Gen 1.1—In the beginning God

created the world was without form
and void. Had no shape just water forever,
no land just sitting in and on the water world
without end or edge.

Even though there are end-stops in the poem, the poem as a whole
does not stop. Instead, it spirals, it rhymes, it enjambs, it slides diag-
onally across the page, and—as the concluding line pivots back up
alongside its penultimate—off it. Even here, even when he's supposed to die, he won't.

he's a knight and that's a dragon and this is why I fight
this no matter what happens I'll go right on fighting
even now with everything in a shambles they thought
even the firemen thought we've got you this time you
bastard you can't go on from this but I'll stick on

I: Right

CJ: Stay right here

I: Right

CJ: Fight the dragons

XII. Legend[12]

XIII. Boundaries

"A heroic epic, truly such, is undoubtedly the greatest work
which the soul of man is capable to perform. . . . The action of
it is always one, entire, and great."

> (John Dryden, *Dedication of the
> Aeneis: To the Most Honourable
> John, Lord Marquess of Normandy,
> Earl of Mulgrave, and Knight of the
> Most Noble Order of the Garter,* Ox-
> ford: Clarendon Press, 1697)

---

[12] *Once upon a time the world begot giants after sleeping with Pride,
but when their god looked down and howled at them, then the world
bowed its head below floodmarks and then drowned.*

"'He whose corpse in desert lieth,
Hast thou seen him?' '(Aye), I saw;
Not in earth doth rest his spirit.'
'He whose ghost hath none to tend,
Didst thou see him?' '(Aye), I saw,
Lees of cup, and broken bread
Thrown into the street he eateth.'"   (C. 2000 B.C.)

> (Anon., *The Epic of Gil-
> gamish: A New Transla-
> tion from a Collation of
> the Cuneiform Tablets in
> the British Museum Ren-
> dered Literally into En-
> glish Hexametres,* trans.
> R. Campbell Thompson,
> M.A., D.Litt., F.S.A., Lon-
> don: Luzac Co., 1740)

"She spoke, and the heart of Odysseus was glad to obey.
Then Pallas Athena, daughter of aegis-bearing Zeus,
She who appeared like a Mentor in form and voice,
Made a sacred, and lasting, covenant between them."
(C. 700 B.C.)

> (Homer, *The Odyssey: For the
> Right Honourable Countess
> Dowager Spencer, the Follow-
> ing Being a Translation of the
> Odyssey, a Poem That Exhib-
> its in the Character of Its*

Heroine an Example of All Domestic Virtue, Is With Equal Propriety and Respect Inscribed by His Ladyship's Most Devoted Servant, the Author, trans. William Cowper, London: J.M. Dent, 1910)

"Then Turnus went slack
In his arms and his legs with the chill of death, and his life
Fled with a groan indignantly down to the shadows."   (19)

(Virgil, *The Aeneid: A Translation by Richard Stanyherst with Other Poetical Devices Thereto Annexed,* Westminster: Archibald Constable and Co., 1895)

"For my part, I give this warning to everyone
    who is listening to the words of prophecy in this book:
    should anyone add to them,
    God will add to him the plagues described in this book;
should anyone take away from the
    words in this book of prophecy,
    God will take away from him
    his share in the tree of life and the holy city,
described herein."   (c. 90)

(St. John, "The Revelation of John," *A Bible for the Liberal,* New York: Library Press, 1946)

"My Guide and I took that funereal
	path which leads back to a world all glittering.
	Nor did we care for any rest at all,
but laboured up—he first—I following—
	till I could glimpse those gorgeous calendars
	the Heaven's display, through a round opening
whence we came out: once more we saw the stars."   (1310)

> (Dante Alighieri, *Inferno: With Translations Broadcast in the B.B.C. Third Programme*, trans. Terence Tiller, England: Curwen Press, 1966)

"With dreadful faces thronged and fiery arms
Some natural tears they dropped, but wiped them soon;
The world was all before them, where to choose
Their place of rest, and Paradise their guide;
Thy hand in hand with wand'ring steps and slow,
Through Eden took their solitary way."   (1667)

> (John Milton, *Paradise Lost: Containing His Poetical Works with Plans for Other Tragedies*, London: Bye and Law, 1801)

"Perhaps, in this case, a poem might help enlighten the
	reader:—
	God of the night, at whose voice

The tired sun makes haste to set,
And, like a giant, hath rejoiced
    To run his journey through the skies
Commands the sun once more be down!
    To lull the earth and chill the ground." (1873)

(Rowbotham, "General Sum-
mary, Application, & Cui
Bono," *Earth Not a Globe*)

"Vladimir: Well? Shall we go?
Estragon: Yes, let's go.
They do not move." (1952)

(Samuel Beckett, *Waiting for
Godot*, London: Faber and
Faber, 1952)

"'Sal, we gotta go and never stop going till we get there.'
'Where we going, man?'
'I don't know, but we gotta go.'" (1957)

(Jack Kerouac, *On the Road*,
New York: Viking, 1957)

XIV. Seconds

I: When did all this happen sir

CJ:

I: All this fallen human stuff

CJ:

I: All your work without the

CJ:

I: All your words without their

CJ:

I: All this fallen human stuff

XV. Legend[13]

(Areas Not Shown)

* To the west is ocean

* East are many mountains

* You may encounter construction and delays on Freeway 14

* Highway 5 is closed

* Where the road narrows use lights and horn

* Where there is smoke there is fire

* This border is where patrol is most heavy

* Not all points of interest are marked

* Where it says gas read faith

---

[13] *Once upon a time the world erected stone towers toward heaven, but when their god looked down and howled at them, then the world turned frail as clay dust and then spread.*

* Where it says faith read with caution

* Where you see smile think end of road

* (Ditto for tea, wave, photo, sun . . .)

* Where you think you get it, turn

* Where you think you don't, turn

* Not all points of interest are marked

* Where I tried to indicate "I" I used the word *I*; for "you" I used *you*; "he," *he;* et cetera

* Names of persons and places have been changed unless otherwise noted

* Trees, towers, and water should remain trees, towers, and water, except in those cases when I mean death

* When I say death don't roll your eyes

* I think sometimes the world is what has been departing

* Yes I mean it watch out where you go

* There are times I feel when even essays fail. They break down

* And then where are you? Think of something you believe in then

* Kill it; think of something big. An essay that becomes a lyric

* Is an essay that has killed itself. I don't mean it like that

* Exactly. I mean that everything you then do to try to save that

* Essay—be it breadth, numbers, quotes, footnotes

* Etc.—will only make it elegy for what it's

* Not

* Where it says legend, read I told you so
* Where it says let, read dare
* Where it says maybe he will live forever, you should know
  that he did not

Door No. Four

The Wonders of Galvanism and Its Applications; The Wonders of Geology: Or, a Familiar Exposition of Geological Phenomena; The Wonders of Geyserland: Yellowstone National Park; The Wonders of Glass-Making in All Ages; Goats; God in the Wilderness; God's Creation Manifested; The Golden West: Being a Graphic Elucidation of a Thousand Marvelous Spectacles Witnessed in Crossing the Continent in a Palace Car; The Great Barrier Reef; The Great City: The Sins of New York; The Great Deep; The Great Mammoth Cave of Kentucky; The Great Unveiling: A Remarkable Book of Revelation; Grace in Russia; Gravity; Growing Plants.

The Hawk World; Heat and Light; The Heavens: Being a Popular View of Astronomy, Including a Full Illustration of the Mechanism of the Heavens; His Grace; The Wonders of Hobby-

craft; The Wonders of Home; How Animals Learn; Human Bodies; Hummingbirds.

The Wonders of Insect Life; Of Instinct; The Invincible; The Invisible World: Being an Account of the Tryals of Several Witches Lately Executed in New England; The Wonders of the Invisible World: Together with Notes and Explanations; The Wonders of Ireland: A Personal Choice of 484; Italy.

Japan: A Portfolio of Views in the Enchanted Bamboo-Land.

The Kenya Seashore: A Short Guide; The Kept Woman; The Kingdom: A Study of the Miracles of Jesus; Korea.

Light and Color; Life on Earth; Lions; The Little World: A General History of Man, Displaying the Various Faculties, Capacities, Powers and Defects of the Human Body and Mind; The Wonders of Llamas; The Wonders of Load-Stones.

Hall of Fame:
An Essay About the Ways
in Which We Matter

> . . . I herde a gret noise withalle
> In a corner of the halle,
> Ther men of love tydings tolde,
> And I gan thiderward behold;
> For I saugh renninge every wight,
> As faste as that they hadden might;
> And everich cryed, "What thing is that?"
> And some seyde, "I not never what."
> And whan they were alle on an hepe,
> Tho behind gonne up lepe,
> And clamben up on othere heles
> And stampe, as men don after eles.
> Atte laste I saugh a man,
> Which that I nevene naught ne can;
> But he seemed for to be
> A man of great Auctoritee . . .

Unfinished.
> (Geoffrey Chaucer,
> *The Hous of Fame*)

Fifteen Ways:
An Introduction to the Hall of Fame:
An Essay About the Ways in Which We Matter

(1)

Asked whether or not he was afraid to die, William Blake, on his deathbed, said: ". . . as afraid as I might be if I were to walk into the next room."

(2)

Earlier than this, but still on that bed, it was William Blake who also said: "There are things known and things unknown and between them are the doors."

(3)

That is the place we are in.

You and I and the road.

(4)

One of us idling in the museum parking lot.

One of us up the museum steps goes.

For a very long time I am in there, gone.

You are sitting and idling, really wanting to go.

(5)

Gone.

(6)

Inside, meanwhile, on my side of the wall, Andy Warhol's *Deaths* fill the gallery's white height.

Every record-skip red.

Every jagged shot same.

Every single one of those hundred-eight frames.

(7)

Later, in the archives, a woman is chewing gum.

"Shh!" she whispers, from her cubicle into mine, "we're not supposed to talk, but let me just say—

"Andy liked to buy a new record everyday.

"He would play it in the morning, play it all night, learn it, love it, then throw it away.

"He got bored very quickly.

"Went out and got another.

"The whole process starting all over.

He was a hard man to know. . . ."

(8)

Outside, on the other side, walls are what make Pittsburgh rise.

All its steely beaks clutch heavenward.

All its up-and-at-'em stacks.

(9)

I grew up, I do not think it is specious to point out, in a home without a hall.

Mother, Brother, and I lived together in a basement studio apartment.

Boston.

We would watch the sun as it snuck past our window on sneakers and wing tips and pumps everyday.

(10)

At night, Brother and I got folded into a futon beneath the window.

Mother into a large walk-in closet beside the door.

(11)

Together we, the three souls, lay—watching as the ceiling lowered and leaned.

(12)

It was something perfectly quiet.

I, for example, would dream.

(13)

Quiet.

(14)

Our heads tossing not.

Our tiny room square.

Our bruise-deepened sky.

(15)

We were going nowhere.

FAMILY CAMPING HALL OF FAME
ALLENTOWN, NEW HAMPSHIRE

That night we lay scattered among the clover, trying to sleep, trying to hold tightly to the ground, holding our breaths so as not to propel ourselves, or each other, off and onto the lance-high peaks of elsewhere.

I watched the sky.

There are parts of it we are meant to connect.

Show which.

Hall of Fame of You
Athens, Greece

I

One night in Athens, on bus 64 to the port of Pireus, a graying man with paling skin explained to me the Greek transit system.

Metaphor, he called it.

Trains, buses, the gondolas up north, we Greeks go nowhere without one.

Modes of transportation are *metaphor,* and so is the act of traveling *metaphor,* and on good days parliamentary proceedings can be *metaphorical,* too, he explained.

Paused.

Tried to take my hand.

In ancient times, he then recalled, philosophers and playwrights and rhetoricians around these parts thought of love as many balls.

Those couples in love roamed, rolling across greens and pastures.

Those of us out of love—lopsided—walked.

We, the ancient balls insist, search through life for long-lost halves.

Pause.

You are driving to the sea? You are sailing on to Crete? he asked. I would like to rent a cabin but they are held for only pairs. You do read me? Catch the drift? I have tried, my friend, tried, I say, renting cabins on my own, but always—always, understand—the agents, they will not sell.

For 52,000 drachmas we sailed to Crete.

A bargain, I wrote home that night.

Cabins being rare in Greece.

Only held for pairs.

II

If you read me, do you love me?

Plato wants to know.

In *Phaedrus,* in *Symposium,* in *Timaeus,* he wants to know.

I am looking at a life-sized marble statue of Apollo—big doughy curls, small angled waist, feet in a plinth—but cannot tell you.

". . . all of this, combined with the statue's hazy acquisition, makes this 'alleged' Greek kouros difficult to authenticate, or even read, Hellenic researchers claim," the J. Paul Getty Museum explains.

What we know for certain is that the Greek kouros was popular in its day.

It inspired many new forms of art, including, among them, several previously unexpressed expressions of loving one's self described rather boldly on red-figure vases.

So beautiful the ancients found the kouros, in fact, that mounted guards stood post around its temple in order to face-off large crowds at noon, which, otherwise, without restraint, would have risked dismembering the statue by overwhelming it from the rear, ancient sources tell us.

III

More statues were carved, more Greeks fell in love, 615–460 B.C.

IV

This is before Plato arrived with Ideals.

This is before Love left with Plato.

In 1983 the Getty Museum purchased this kouros because, we suspect, someone fell in love.

In 1984 the Greek government called a conference.

"A fake."

"Dishonest."

"Mistake," they called it.

Why?

Are human beings with the ability to fall in love with statues human beings who need not read Plato?

V

Beautiful marble you.

Now that we are captive on a ship, now that we have captured Love—

Lunch?

Nap?

A lap around the bed?

The tiny circle sea.

What are we doing after dinner, sir? What are we doing after that?

And then what?

And then, what?

Are you planning to stroll around the deck with me?

Are we planning to share this bed?

These are things I need to know.

As well as:

When will it be arriving, sir?

That thing I *made* you for?

Does it help if I say "beautiful"?

Any more if I say "marble"?

What about *irreparable?* Or *borrowed?*

Forever?

Lent?

How close will we ever get?

How close do we have to get?

Do you have to touch me?

Do I have to say something?

Should I be dressed?

Should you be "she"?

I thought all I had to do was write.

I thought something was supposed to happen.

MAGIC HALL OF FAME
ST. LOUIS, MISSOURI

They're still mourning.

A year past his death.

The hungry Harry Houdini fans have picked off huge locks from his Traveling Trunk No. 8.

Have found, inside, cans.

Metal, wood, and cardboard containers, each wrapped in a pelt, alphabetically arranged, rubbed into cold white glints and flames, full of the polished secrets of his fame—

All his milk cans: the "Challenge Can," the "Chinese Torture Can," "Detroit Can," "New York Can," "can, 1910, unprepared."

Can of corn kernels, can of keys, can of Wohmung's Sealing and Other Waxes.

Of chalk, crayons, jeweler's rouge.

Of thread, buttons, paint brushes.

An oil can, a caulking can, spirit gum, and putty cans.

Cans of lock picks, cans of glass tools, cans of five planes, hammers and mallets.

Grindstone cans and spokeshave cans.

Dividers with calipers and files in a can.

(In a sailcloth sack near the back of the trunk, Fred T. Hodgson's *The ABCs of the Steel Square and Its Uses*, 1908.)

A can slightly dented.

Can of four vices.

Can for wrenches, pliers, and pullers.

One for axes, one for leather.

Five used abrasive papers rolled in a can.

His notepad for tricks tucked between two cans.

(His "SHOULD," his "SHOULDN'T HAVE," his "HAZARDOUS MAYBE."

In longhand, fans tell us, Harry's hand says *can!*)

And chisels and scrap wood and half-whittled sea serpents—which breach, have been breaching, will still be breaching when we are done mourning, when the Trunk is packed up, when it's gone into storage—from these four metal cans of balsa-wood blocks.

How much longer do we have till they rot?

Hall of Fame of Me
Cambridge, Massachusetts

I wonder why I don't dream anymore, the donor is thinking.

What languages I speak.

What animals I like.

To where I would want to travel and why.

He inserts his left palm into the black plastic box.

Waits.

The receptionist waves him in.

On full green sofas along the walls the donors wait with *Sport* on their laps.

With *People,* and *Men's Health,* and *Details,* and *Time.*

How would the donor describe his personality?

In what condition are his teeth?

Does he have hobbies?

Talents?

In youth, what color was his grandfather's hair?

A cake comes into the room.

The icing on it blue.

WAY TO GO! 18 MONTHS! 5-0-7 YEAH!

Donor 5-0-7 sits with cake and says that eighteen months might sound like long, but really it's just a year and a half.

The donors lick their fingers.

Nod.

Remember to ask about our Bonus Program, the woman on the poster reminds the donors, surfboard between her legs:

You get $$$ when your friend applies. More $$$ if he qualifies!

She licks her lips. The donors lick. The woman closes her eyes.

You know, says donor 5-0-7, this is what I call *the life!*

The donors chuckle.

Continue licks.

Does he have a favorite color?

He should explain so here.

Shuffleboard Hall of Fame
St. Petersburg, Florida

("Renovations made possible by Anderson–McQueen
Funeral Housing and Cremation Services—
Conveniently Located in Your Neighborhood!")

Are those your bones I hear rattling across the terrazzo, sir, or
are you challenging me to a game?

Billiards Hall of Fame
Brooklyn, New York

Pool makes the unlikely sexy.

When you break like that, when you feather, I find this very sexy.

I find chalking sexy.

Blowing it.

I find myself often hanging off the TV, ogling those grease-balls who spin spheres like Apollo.

Don't let them tell you Mozart died writing a requiem.

Pool sharks and prostitutes on every street corner knew him.

Even Cleopatra—that old hustler—scratched her way from the grave to seduce Shakespeare.

"Let's to billiards," she declares, in Act 2.

Yet she always winds up dead.

What I want is the two of us tucked between their epitaphs—secretive, squirreled, pocketed behind tombstones.

I know rackfuls of sunken moons.

So cue up tonight. Sink into me.

Do not scratch.

Not even touches.

Living History Hall of Fame, II
9th Massachusetts Light Artillery Camp, Vermont

Marching through the cold, green, tent-pitched mountains of old Vermont at 6 A.M. while clumps of wind go hurling against the birch-stalk stands, go bouncing and pelting the Hogback River, flinging us both toward dawn, I have been thinking about what makes him tick, about what ticks.

Let us cross over the river, he says, and rest under the shade of the trees.

Father, lying under the bough of a dark holm-oak—clicking and clicking and nailing down the day—has come to watch me write about a war.

"The war," say sandwich boards strewn across the battlefield, "that everyone fought, all of us won, here, on this day, on hallowed ground, where brother v. brother v. father v. son . . ."

What is it that comes after a long civil war?

Where we are, it is summer.

There is hanging around his neck a small black camera, and it ticks.

Want to make some money off of this? my father says. You just find a few good anecdotes. Click.

And it's summer.

First time together in fifteen years.

Click.

There are rifle fires, and we hear them.

Troops advance, and we point.

Smoke from cannons curls a quick bow over the valley—but blows away, soon.

Blowing a long sigh out from under the shade of some trees.

Blowing a few hoopskirts like bells across the river.

Blowing off hats, blowing down tents.

Blowing past the rubber banner PEPSI CIVIL WAR EVENT HERE.

Then blowing onto cars slowed down for HAIRPIN TURN.

USE HORN.

But up, over the valley, under the low-roofed pitch of Exhibit Hall A, I can see no smoke.

See: only the flags folded, and the wagon hitched, and the two dozen coffee urns, and the old vendor selling glass she cut from the greenhouse panes of an old Victorian.

Glass, the vendor claims, which someone, long ago, after the war was done, purchased in bulk from the bankrupt Mathew Brady.

Whose six thousand negatives of soldiers who survived the war were no longer necessary, no longer "right."

They were leaded instead into windows in New England.

Then made positive again.

Then bleached clear by the weather.

LIVING HISTORY HALL OF FAME, I
STORY LAND PARK, NEW HAMPSHIRE

He's the camera, I'm the pose. In this photograph I am *happy.*

*

He's the giant, I'm the bean. In this one, I am *climbing.*

*

One of us wants *up, up.*

*

The other, *Don't make me come down there.*

*

His the voice like cannons booming down the stalk.

*

I, the clouds like smoke, clear.

*

An axe.

*

I will make this story clear enough.

*

He's the angle of the shot as if climbing—*I'm chasing you!*—
down.

*

I'm the pose underneath him—*Look guilty, now!*
Swing your axe!
You're angry, son. Angry!

*

In which photograph am I happy?

*

One of us will break his crown today.

*

One of us will live forever.

*

(If the park doesn't close first.)

*

(If his story *wants* an end.)

*

He's the wind-clicks come hard against the stalk.

*

I'm the chicken wire, the fiberglass, the green leaves of the stalk.

*

Have I made this story clear enough?

*

Tell me, please, if I need to be scared. If the sky is worth it. If the *up* is smart.

*

You know this story well.

*

Enough, then:

*

Tell me, now, your gold harp in hand, wind strumming down the broad-leaf boughs of the stalk, what sounds they make— my imaginary chops—and who clicks the photograph when our bough finally breaks.

ROUTE 66 HALL OF FAME
McLean, Illinois

We are standing outside a truck stop on opposite sides of a red neon ROUTE 66 HALL OF FAME sign after having sat all night, and some of the morning, in a booth, in the diner inside, arguing about Las Vegas.

I am "Viva!" Las Vegas, and you are "Not viva!," and for this I am also "Perverse."

This was yesterday.

We went into the Hall, ate omelettes, and are six hours later exiting into today.

I am sorry. I should have warned you about the Hall's substancelessness.

How the meaning you like to find inside a thing would most likely be rotten here.

(See that girl half our age jumping out a truck's cab and hopping into the next?)

Paul Bunyan, I agree, surely had it better off in 1968 when he was carrying lumber along Route 66 for the Johnson Timber Company in Dixie.

Look at him in these recent photographs, however, and tell me what is so perverse about Paul, here in Wilmington, carrying a pile of hot dogs like lumber.

Or Paul, in Cicero, carrying a pile of tires like lumber.

Or Paul, now in Springfield, in fresh silver paint, carrying from the entrance of Launching Pad Drive-In a pile of moon rocks like lumber.

Halls are like this, elegiac.

After time, however, even they will signify nothing at all but themselves.

Like now, standing beside you glowing—

I am watching you eyeing this neon sign, reading the sticker placed, either conspicuously or inconspicuously, on the large black motor aloud:

"Outlaw Neon," you read.

(A protest.)

"Outlaw Neon," I read.

(A company.)

It's so much like you, I think, to find action in things.

You must excuse me, though, if I don't make a move.

I tend to love foremost the thing.

Big Daddy's Drag Racing Hall of Fame
Ocala, Florida

One day in 1980, as the USS *Ranger* maneuvered slowly through navy drills in the perpetual blue sprawl of the Pacific Ocean, Big Daddy's dragster raced an F-14 jet down the floating runway, and won.

How?

Big Daddy believes in humans.

Big Daddy has human dreams.

"If God had meant for man to stay put in the living room, He'd have kept speed to Himself," Big Daddy says, boldly blending hydrogen and silver for fuel.

Peering past the aircraft carrier's runway that day, Big Daddy sees an infinite potential for speed.

Infinite, he thinks.

Just no runway.

Museum of American Frontier Culture
and Hall of Fame
Staunton, Virginia

But what you should concentrate on is my homesickness.

All these road maps, tickets, things-in-a-glass case—

What could make you homesick? For what drive until you glimpsed an end?

Look: here they have a little Pilgrim village, a little farming lot, a small extravaganza of skirmishes.

EVERY HOUR, WEATHER WILLING, the Indians appear, run around, yell, set fire, raid, pretend to kill a young lady, leave.

Every evening with flax the young lady attaches whatever she wants to happen next onto the soaked-blank flour sacks, then waits.

The Indians appear. The Indians leave.

Flax, and now the gown taking shape there, where the collar soon, the insinuation of a sleeve . . .

The Indians there, not there.

The sacks soaked free of their stamped-on trademarks.

The flax soaked up by the gown as it stretches.

The sacks undone into windows of flowers.

Or maybe filigree.

Or are they fringes?

(The Indians continuing to visit her.)

Stop here and it is *wedding dress*. Stop here and it is *tablecloth*.

What do you want to see? Say where you want to go.

I want to come to a full-stop place eventually.

Want to see you looking here, and catch myself looking back, and find between us a distance, after all, that is not so great.

And not so insignificant.

AMERICAN RIVERS HALL OF FAME
DUBUQUE, IOWA

Think:

Mark Twain, "Irony never made it over the Mississippi."

Full-throttle then. 1819. Four men go voyaging the Upper Mississippi.

Botanist, anthropologist, geographer, and painter—the four edges of our net cast deep into the river.

River cast as the world.

On it, the four men are straddling a steaming sea serpent, constructed for them by the Diamond Joe Steamboat Line, Hannibal, Missouri.

This way, they think, the savages along the riverbanks will recoil as the monster swims upstream, black scales on her hull, red tail like a rudder, fire-breathing prow.

Word spreads wildly along the thickening banks.

Spreads so thick with savages one night that the crew swings port to elude them.

Port, then over.

And the savages, then gathering evening's wood on small birch mats, fear the serpent will engorge her captors.

So they throw their white life preservers into the moonless river.

At this, however, the men recoil.

They swim back toward their retreating steamboat.

Cramp yards away from the watching savages.

Drown feet beneath the moon-ivory mats.

American Hall of Famous Ventriloquists
Las Vegas, Nevada

"I am tired of the old stones," said my host.

"I want all things clean again.

"I want my dinner to be midnight, and the sun still to be shining."

My host's wife caught my eyes as she smiled.

Patted her husband's back.

He blushed, looked down at his glass.

A waiter came.

My host ordered *prosciutto e melone.*

His wife, *Caffè per favore.*

All around were stone façades.

Tourist crowds.

The famous four-rivers fountain by Bernini.

The sky swirled quietly on its flat firmament.

In the water, there were coins, and an undeveloped Polaroid.

Cool air blew in from unseen shores.

Soothing music played.

Someone swept up trash with a broom.

A toast.

"For seven months every year," said my host, "I am in Belgium freelance anesthesiologist.

"The rest of the time I tour this world.

"Tasting of cuisine."

There was some commotion then from the kitchen.

My host put down his glass.

A teenaged boy came screaming out.

A dining table got kicked askew.

Place settings spread all out of place.

A guard nearby at the Disney Store radioed for backup.

And it came.

American Police Hall of Fame
Miami, Florida

José Manuel Miguel Xavier Gonzales, in a few short weeks it will be spring. The snows of winter will flee, the ice will vanish, the air will become soft and balmy. In short, José Manuel Miguel Xavier Gonzales, the annual miracle of years will come to pass, yet you will not be here to enjoy it. The rivulet will run its soaring course to sea, the timid desert flowers will put forth their tender shoots, the glorious valleys of this imperial domain will blossom like a rose. But you will not be here. From every treetop some wild songster will carol his mating song. Butterflies will sport in sunshine, the busy bee will hum happily as it pursues its accustomed vocation. The gentle breeze shall tease the tassels of wild grasses, and all of nature, José Manuel Miguel Xavier Gonzales, will be glad but you. You will not be here to enjoy it because I command hereby the sheriff of this town to lead you out to some remote location, swing you by your neck from the bough of a knotting oak, and let you hang there until you are dead. And then, José Manuel Miguel Xavier Gonzales, I command furthermore that such officers retire quickly from your dangling corpse, that the sun burn hot, that vultures then descend from the heavens upon your filthy body, so that nothing, José Manuel Miguel Xavier Gonzales, shall remain of you but the chill, bare, bleached bones of a cold-blooded, copper-colored, blood-thirsty, throat-cutting, chili-eating, sheep-herding, murdering son-of-a-bitch.

(Judge Roy Bean, U.S. District Court, New Mexico Territory Sessions, 1881, Hall of Fame Inductee)

National Cowboy Hall of Fame and Western Heritage Museum of Freedom *
Oklahoma City, Oklahoma

We . . . doe by these presents solemnly & mutually in ye presence of God, and one of another, covenant & combine our selves togeather into a civill body politick; for our better ordering & preservation & furtherance of ye ends aforesaid . . .

(Mayflower Compact, 1620)

. . . the fulfillment of our manifest destiny is to overspread the continent allotted by Providence for the free development of our yearly multiplying millions.

(*United States Magazine and Democratic Review*, 1845)

My forefathers didn't come over on the *Mayflower*, but they did meet the boat.

(Will Rogers, 1924)

---

*

Stover's Star
Crandal's Zigzag
Crandal's Alternating Barb Strip
Schuman's Double Edged Saw Tooth Slat
Cloud's Barbed Warning Strip
Preston's Braid
Meriwether's Cold Weather Wire

Reynold's Web

Brock's Take Up Knot

Govenor's Loop and Bend Ornamental Fencing

Shellaberger's Loops

Shellaberger's Spaced Loops

Shellaberger's Zigzag

Shellaberger's Long Zigzag

Shellaberger's Snake Wrap

Cleaveland's Weave and Twist

Riter's Corrugated Visible Wire

Cleaveland's Weave

Wright's Ornamental Wire

Cleaveland's Spiral Twist Walking Wire

Loop and Hitch Ornamental Wire

Miles' Barbless Parallel

Miles' Barbless Wide Parallel

Miles' Barbless Three Strand Parallel

Hathaway-Woodward's Ornamental

Hathaway-Woodward's Ornamental Weave Wire

Hathaway-Woodward's Ornamental Weave Edge Wire

Hathaway-Woodward's Ornamental Twist Edge Wire

Woodward's Ornamental Loops

Ingrahm's Visible Loop Wire Fencing

Curtis's Ladder

Curtis's Ladder With Slat

Riter's Visible Lace Wire

Cleaveland's Half Loop Visible Wire Fencing

Cleaveland's Full Loop Visible Wire Fencing

Cleaveland's Undulating Visible Wire Fencing

Cleaveland's Zigzag Visible Wire Fencing

McNelly's Wide Loop
McNelly's Single Loops
McNelly's Pull Through Loop
Smith's Rings
Riter's Visible Wire
Smith's Zigzag Spread
Smith's Spread Zigzag and Arch
Smith's Square
Smith's Descending Beads
Smith's Double Oval Variation
Miles' Knife Edge
Miles' One Strand Open Diamond Point
Miles' Double Strand Open Diamond Point
Miles' Closed Diamond Point
Big John
Great Taper Barb
Stover's Single Wrap Barb
Dobb's Grooved Fence Wire
Miles' Staple Barb
Haish's Grooved Wire and Crimped Barb
Baker's One Strand Barb
Brock's Barbed Take Up Knot
Baker's Hanging Square Strand Knot
Glidden's Hanging Coil Barb Variation
Glidden's Flattened Strand Coil Variation
Glidden's One Strand Hanging Variation
Decker's Ribbed Fence Wire with Wire Barb
Glidden's Twist Oval
Glidden's Twist Oval, Light Duty Variation
Upham's Round Strand Coil

Upham's Half-Round Strand Coil
Upham's Twist Oval Strand Coil Variation
Lenox's Single Knob Fence Wire
Haish's Wide Spaced
Haish's Ribbed Corrugated Wire
Haish's Wide-Spread Smooth Wire Barb
Roger's Wire with Coil Barb
Roger's Non-Slip Straight Barb Variation
Miller's Splint Barb
Rose's Wide-Wrap Barb
Rose's Wide-Wrap One Strand Barb Variation
Doerr's Electric Fence Wire
Smith's Edge-Drilled Warning Block Brab
Smith's Side-Drilled Warning Block Barb
Smith's Notched Two Point Warning Block Barb
Sunderland's Straight Strand Barb Variation
Mighell's Winding One Strand Barb
Daley's Long Wrap
Daley's Caduceus
Brigg's Snake Wire and Spiral Barb
Dobbs-Booth's Non-Slip Staple Barb
Emerson's Loop
Scutt's Four Point Tie
Shinn's Barb
Upham's Crossed Loops
Hill's Caged Barb
Decker's Wire and Plate
Upham's Loop and Lock
Briggs' Locked "S"
Gunderson's Trapped Barb

Edenborn's Double Strand Wrapped Barb
Curtis' Cross Lock
Curtis' Loop Lock
Curtis' Cross Jumbo Hook Lock Variation
Curtis' Cross Modern Plastic Coat Lock Variation
Curtis' Cross Hook Lock Variation
Allen's Double Strand Twist Variation
Randall's Caged Barb
McFarland's Caged Barb
Washburn's Twist
Lenox's Twist
Winterbotham's Caged Barb
Ford's Kink and Double Twist and Strand Barb
Duncan's Double Strand and Triple Twist Tie
Jayne-Hill's Double Strand Barb
Jayne-Hill's Double Strand Barb Variation
Scutt's Locked Rings
St. John's Locked Double Strand Staples
Wing's Double Staple Variation
Billing's Simple
Steven's "X"
Upham's Loop and Lock Single Bend Variation
Bodham's Matched Loops
Bodham's Opposed Loops
Randel's Interlocking Staples
Ellwood's Parallel and Tied Twist
Edenborn-Grische's Cross Barbs
Curtis' Split Half Round
Mouck's Three-to-One Parallel Strand Barb
Hodge's Wire Rowel

Delff's Leaf
Brotherton's Flat Wire Variation
Brink's Notched Double Strand Plate
Brink's Double Strand Butt Plate
Brainerd's Double Strand Sleeve and Strap
Nadelhoffer's Flat-Wire Gull Wing
Kelly's Thorny Double Strand Fence
Kelly's Thorny Common Fence Variation
Kelly's Thorny Mixed Barb Fence Variation
Gregg's Bow and Perforated Strip
De Walt's Diamond
Upham's Diamond with Anchor Lugs
Scutt's Crimp Flat Wire Barb Variation
Armstrong-Doolittle's Notched Diamond
Haish's Grooved Wire and Ribbed Barb
Upham's Screw Barb
Griswold's Ribbed Barb
Griswold's Center-Core Barb
Griswold's Fastener
Barr's Two Point Plate Barb
Sergeant's Barb Plate
Smith's Blunt Point Barb Plate
Stover's Corsicana Clip Barb
Haish's Anvil Barb
Haish's Horn Barb
Kelly's Grooved Pin
May's Bar Bell
Dodge's Knobby Barb
Brink's Three Point Long Plate
Brink's Variation . . .

Hall of Fame of Us
Rachel, Nevada

("The Extraterrestrial Highway")

Ergo the town.

Also the fence.

Most of Rachel, Nevada, lives near this fence.

Come dusk, at the Little Ale'Inn, the town gets drunk on talk about the fence.

So-and-so peeping over the fence.

Such-and-such sneaking around the fence.

The fence and the blight of fascist American conspiracies.

Etc.

On the other side, at night, sometimes a white Jeep stalks the desert, sometimes a black jet zips the sky.

Always in bunkers and warehoused in vaults, alien captives are crying out.

If we could only get inside of Area 51, say the townspeople of Rachel—population 91—we could save the aliens, and thus save ourselves.

In the meantime, at least, we know that they are near.

We know, for example, of five ships docked on the other side, though we have our suspicions of six.

We know of two bunkers above ground, innumerable bunkers below.

We know Roswell, Atlantis, Bermuda Triangle . . .

We know that they are kind.

They want to take us with them.

We know a lot, in fact. Just not enough.

Not, at least, till we're on the other side.

Visiting the bar one early afternoon, I asked the waitress what she'd recommend.

"Alienburger."

No doubt about it.

"It's a green-dyed patty," she said.

"Green?"

"Don't worry, hon," the waitress said.

"It's not real alien meat," she added.

"Real alien meat, of course, is greener!"

U.S. Astronaut Hall of Fame
Titusville, Florida

The Choco Indians live on another moon.

The one on the other side of Tranquility.

Curious about this place, NASA asked the Choco to tell them more about their soppy days, their elephant moths, and about the western peaks they call "the jaws," which astronauts mistake for horizon.

Researching the Choco with utmost care, NASA assessed their world in a report called "Survival"—manual 64–5 in astronaut training.

In it, also, are Protestant, Catholic, and Jewish prayers.

Liturgical readings.

Emergency burial ministrations.

Even more than blasting off, even more than fiery deaths, NASA fears a rocket launching their men into the gaps that exist between civilizations.

Fastidiously they plot the route there for every new astronaut.

"See?"—

NASA says, "Don't go there."

The astronauts memorize this route, and then forget it.

In their minds a thought the size of a jungle, only empty, remains.

We call this space.

HALL OF FAME OF THEM
RACHEL, NEVADA

One-half of one of these thirty-five trailers hitched beside the Little Ale'Inn is available for rent to any stranger.

That's us.

For thirty-one dollars: dinner tonight.

Air-conditioning.

Breakfast.

All the videos we want.

Videos? I ask.

"Darling, where do you think you are?" the waitress asks.

"TV reception sucks to high heaven out here.

"The only time it's not bad is when something flies overhead."

Tonight the early bird is T-bone steak.

Corn.

Roll.

Mashed or fries.

We are watching—we five early birds in Rachel tonight—the owner of the Little Ale'Inn on *Larry King*.

"So you thought, 'Heck, if this thing ever happens to me again,'" says Larry live, "'then next time I'm gonna to be prepared!'"

"Right," says the owner.

"So you did what?"

"I bought insurance."

"She bought insurance, ladies and gentlemen!"

The first American to be covered for abductions.

"Bet now we're gonna need more help," the cashier predicts, folding black T-shirts with gold saucer contrails:

RACHEL, EARTH!

A commercial comes on.

The kitchen bell's rung.

Someone gets up and goes into the closet.

A woman stands up and walks behind the pine bar.

Sits back down with a Bud Light and a Bud.

"So who's going out tonight?" a boy bounds in and starts yelling at the crowd.

"Who's going out 'cause I wanna go out!"

He has been following for the past three nights a certain blue light in the western sky.

"If anyone wants to see it," the teenage boy says, tapping a long finger on my table where he's paused, "no charge!"

"Just promise to let me drive."

Together the teenage boy and I go crashing through the evening sage.

All along the perimeter of Area 51, whizzing metal white posts pass.

"They got, like, miles of bunkers in there," he says.

DO NOT TRESPASS.

GOVERNMENT PROPERTY.

USE OF DEADLY FORCE.

Etc.

"Ships, bodies, you name it."

"Bodies?" I ask. "You've seen bodies?"

"Well, no," says the boy.

"But they're so secret about everything in there, it automatically gives them away."

The best spot for spying on the base's activities has recently been absorbed by a new land ordinance that stretches the government's holdings five miles around the base.

"Hey," he says.

"Yeah?" I say.

"You ever trust anyone that came out just at night?"

"I guess not, no."

"Then why would you trust this government?"

Together we two tear hard into the night in search of a spot from which to spy.

Behind us kicks up dust-red darkness.

Ahead there lifts up nothing from the road.

"I'm telling you—" I start telling him—

"Nothing."

Just the stars in their courses.

Just the moon on its cord.

Just suddenly two guards at the top of the next hill.

We idle.

Paused.

I get out and begin to say:

"Hi.

"We're watching stars.

"Are we on your property?

"I'm very sorry.

"I guess I shouldn't have let my buddy drive.

"Ha!"

The two men wear blue military uniforms.

Berets.

A white Jeep idles beside them.

I see no fence, no line in the sand.

I see that their guns are positioned on their shoulders by black triangular braces.

I see the gun on their white Jeep's roof—

"I'm not from around here.

"See? It's a rental.

"I'm from Boston.

"A tourist!

"Ha!"

Beside the two guards is a white post lit by a spotlight from the Jeep.

THESE GUARDS ARE AUTHORIZED TO REMOVE
ALL INTRUDERS . . . FROM UNITED STATES
GOVERNMENT PROPERTY . . . THIS . . .

                   . . . WITHOUT . . .

. . . PRIOR CLEARANCE . . .

            . . . MILITARY . . .

     . . . CLEARANCE . . .

             . . . TRESPASS ILLEGAL . . .

       . . . BY DEADLY FORCE . . .

. . . THANK YOU.

I stand and look at them.

They stand and aim at me.

On my side of the line are the car's two headlights that stretch a few yards into the night, and end.

On their side of the line: the rest of the night.

Hall of Fame of Groom, Texas
Groom, Texas

"I recall asking the Lord that very same question the morning of my calling, son," Steve Thomas recalled for me under the blue awning of his idling Winnebago Adventurer, idling at the foot of the World's Second Largest Cross, Groom, Texas, at noon.

"'Why Groom, Texas?' I asked the Lord.

"And son, it was at that moment that I remembered the true nature of the Church—that is, to be the Bride of Christ.

"After all, my son, if we the Church become the Bride of Christ, I think then that makes evident what the Lord will be to us!"

I recall sitting under the thick blue awning at Winnebago Adventurer Cross of Our Lord Jesus Christ Church one Tuesday noon in '96, debating whether or not to steal a cassette by Steve Thomas, a two-hour recorded sermon entitled "The Story of Our Cross: God's Marriage to Texans."

But I think, in the end, we'll have to guess what matters.

This tape, for example, just might matter.

The Great State of Texas.

The Second Largest Cross.

Mother leaving Father after only eight months.

I might matter, for all you know, wheeling past fence posts with coyotes strung up like God.

WORLD'S LARGEST PETRIFIED TREE!

HAND-WOVEN RUGS MADE BY REAL INDIANS!

1000s OF POSTCARDS GIFTS SOUVENIRS!

FREE PETRIFIED WOOD TO ALL KIDS UNDER 10!

FOOL'S GOLD REST ROOMS GAS ATM!

Hall of Fame of Every Place You Visit You Must Get a Piece Of
Geronimo, Arizona

(TAKE THIS EXIT!)

Behind the glass counter are two Navajo girls.

The long summer solstice.

Old earth idling in the golden-wide air.

Customers traveling by try the silver rings on.

Copper thimbles.

Beaded jerseys.

Cowboy hats with and without bands.

Meanwhile:

The petrified tree is not getting any younger.

Every day another story comes cashing itself in.

Pulling off the highway.

Loosening rock limbs.

I am there, outside, with the children busy choosing.

PLEASE JUST ONE PIECE OF WOOD PER CHILD
THANX!

It's a long Junish day.

An idle gold width.

The desert at intervals is lunging from us, lurching back.

The children and I rubbish through the green barrels.

They are arranged on the gravel in the shape of a tree.

Inside all the barrels are the fall-apart's pieces.

All its chalky shifting clinks.

I stand there, outside, in the old golden day, and count between the rubbishings how many barrels contain the tree.

(I count sixty.)

But beyond them, behind a fence, an old man with a shovel
points to mounds of more pieces, more tree.

He'll top the barrels off sometime around noon, he says.

"You're giving all this away?"

Still in those mounds, if I stand and count, if I'm willing to
bet, there is a whole generation's worth of pieces left.

With them, he could rebuild the tree.

Or at least its trunk.

Or at the very least a bough.

Gold earth pauses. Starts up again.

Shadows crawling back into the earth crawl out.

"Oh, this ain't the polished stuff," the old man pauses with the shovel and says.

"This stuff is all cheap."

YOU JUST PASSED YOUR LAST CHANCE FOR GOLD!

Oldest Hall of Fame on Earth
Inyo, California

If I had been prepared for this, I'd have said, *The greening light . . . The creak-up green . . . The light.*

But I was not.

This is fame.

What I remember I remember harpooning down the looming mountain, looping round me, pain.

O! let others praise the ancient times, I'm glad I live in these, a modern-minded Ovid wrote.

And then I'm on top of the mountain.

And then uncapping my pen.

And before I know it, the empire's dead.

What I want to remember I remember moaning past the information board at Ancient Bristlecone Pine Forest, then moaning on.

Th   dest   iv g Things   n   rth

it says.

And then a chart to prove the claim.

And then a graph to back the chart.

And above all of this: *Meriwether Lewis*

And: "

Then spread-eagle from YOU ARE HERE goes gravel feathering through the forest patch.

Well, what I say is *gravel,* but nothing so precise is happening.

There are some paths, but more predominant are the gaps around which trees are filing for review.

But even *gap* is something I'm imagining.

Then poking up occasionally, metal pipes.

Bracket latch.

Bolt.

Broken plaque.

Basically, somewhere around here is the oldest living thing on earth.

A tree, they claim.

Or a piece of a tree.

Or some lost refugee from some dead trunk—

They are, perhaps, mere twigs, the living.

But none of them are green.

None of them are anywhere in my scrapbook from this place.

The wind up this mountain pass whips past my car with a whomp.

It hums across the openings of pipes along the path.

It flaps the sign's loose blue paint strips off.

It clinks and rattles this tiny forest.

And hits me.

It hits me:

Here I am.

Start of the world.

Being elsewhere.

Burlesque Hall of Fame
Helendale, California

Finally the place about going almost-all-the-way.

A place locked in the desert still.

A full day's drive to the shore, still.

A dirt road fading into the dirt it cuts through.

Where water's not potable . . .

Sandstorms at noon.

Now that we're stopped, though, why not just stay?

Ask the rest to turn back as we greet them.

Ask them to leave once they have got here, and turn back.

Then, into a light that fades but never quite ends—precisely because we are in the desert still—

we will watch the children, who also will always be children here, carry the fading like painted cloths across the ruts and buttes and long mesa lights.

I want us right here, up against the frontier.

So that I can yell: Children, come home.

August Hall of Fame: An Afterword on Heat
Baker, California

(108/78)

Today is August one.

Nineteen-ninety-eight.

The high today will be one-oh-eight.

The expected low is seventy-eight.

(112/85)

The expected low is higher now.

(112/81)

Today is August three.

(111/84)

I am waiting for a representative from the local chapter of
E Clampus Vitus.

Mr. Daniels, of Baker.

I am expecting him today.

I am in the gateway to the brand-new Mojave National Preserve.

(115/85)

I'm not in the Preserve.

Not out of it.

(117/87)

From the window of my room at the Bun Boy Motel I can see the black highway, the yellow sand nearby, the Bun Boy Restaurant, the Bun Boy Texaco, the desert, its story, its long empty rise.

The World's Tallest Thermometer stands behind me.

Buzz.

(116/85)

Its two thousand amperes.

Its five thousand lamps.

(105/78)

She can't figure it out.

Why, when the ranger, at the information desk inside, checks to log the day's temperature from her government-issued gauge, the mercury-and-glass thermometer and the World's Tallest do not match.

(105/70)

Her expected high is one-oh-one.

It's expecting one-oh-five.

Today is August nine.

(102/69)

When Daniel Gabriel Fahrenheit perfected his scale, he knew that mercury wouldn't cling to glass.

Not even wet the glass.

It races up and down the scale . . .

If we listen, will it sing?

(116/85)

What kind of music did Daniel hear as he worked those days in heat and cold in unpredictable stormy Hague?

He based his new mercury scale on the most stable temperature the world knew of at the time.

The human body's.

96.0 gradi, he wrote.

But what he wrote was off-key.

(103/73)

The first Temple of Mercurius in ancient Rome was built on the Aventine Hill in four-hundred-ninety-five.

Mercury at that time was the god of circulation.

This included overseeing the movement of goods, people, words, and roles.

(107/74)

The same role that Rumor filled when she herself arrived in Rome.

(107/77)

Except Rumor was a Fate, immortal, the evil twin of Fame.

Mercury, in his infancy, was nothing more than divine.

(106/80)

(Now the high has dropped a notch.)

(Now the low has risen?)

(106/79)

Mercury spent those hot wool days in ancient Rome mediating between gods and mortals, racing up and down the scale between dead and living souls, between those in movement and those at rest.

We know that molecules are still when cold.

They're quick when hot.

We know that mercury is the only element that remains a liquid when it's stable.

(105/76)

There are seventy-six thousand eight hundred-twelve pounds of steel in the World's Tallest Thermometer.

Four thousand square feet.

One hundred twenty-five cubic yards of concrete.

Rises one hundred thirty-four feet into the Mojave sky.

One foot for every degree on America's hottest day.

Nineteen-thirteen.

Baker, CA.

(105/79)

Thirty-one people died that day.

This, at least, is what I read in the paper.

(108/78)

As I wait in the Bun Boy I am eating and reading.

Day Trips magazine is complimentary with the meal.

Inside will be suggestions for HIKING WITH YOUR FAM-
ILY! DESERT SAFETY! SHOPPING SHOSHONE!

(110/82)

But it's filled, primarily, with listings for TV.

(111/82)

(There is a good movie at four.)

(There are sports all around.)

(108/77)

You will first taste metal, the excessive production of saliva, teeth loosening, gums blueing, general pain replaced by numbness, then a tendency to withdraw.

Mercury poisoning will inflame intestines.

Will cramp.

Bleed.

(107/79)

Death a possibility.

(108/75)

Still, am waiting.

(109/71)

If you want, you can trace the etymology of *fame* back to "famish," to the Latin word for hunger.

Fames.

A thirst.

But most likely *fame* has its roots in "to speak."

Latin: *Fama.*

The Roman goddess. A Fate in Virgil. Something left lurking in Chaucer's unfinished "Hous of Fame."

(107/71)

Or, if you're hungry, look back even further.

To Lorde Bunne's *Chronicles,* thirteen-thirty-one.

To a place, in our past, where fame itself is starved.

Steuen wille vs traueile, & famen vs to dede.

(106/73)

We know that Mercury's sandals had wings but could not fly.

Do you know that Mercury's sandals could erase immortal footprints?

(105/75)

Today is August.

I am waiting.

A fate has perched outside.

Door No. Five

The Wonders of a Magician's Book of Original Tricks, Concepts, Pictures, Memoirs and Histories; Magic Squares; Magnets and Magnetism; Man: Chateaux of the Loire; The Wonders of Man; The Wonders of Man: Venice; Marsupials; Mathematics; Measurement; Mexico; Mice; The Microscope; Migration; Mines; Modern Chemistry; Modern Architecture; Modern Mechanisms; Modern Medicine; The Modern Rail; The Modern World; The Monkey World; The Moon; The Mosquito World; Mules.

The Natural Mind: The Essence of Dzogchen in the Native Tradition of Tibet; Nature: A Child's First Book About Our Wonderful World; Nature and Art; The New Washington; Norway.

Obligation; An Oceanarium: The Story of Marine Life in Captivity; One-Two-Three; Optics; Organic Life; Our Heritage; Oz.

The Pacific Shore; Parasites; The Past: A World-wide Survey of the Marvelous Works of Man in Ancient Times, Written by Leading Modern Historians; The Past: The Romance of Antique Sculptural Splendors; Peacocks; The Peake; The Pelican World; Physics: An Introduction to Our Physical World; The Piano: Anatomy of an Instrument; Pigs; The Planet Saturn; Plant Life Under a Microscope; Plastic Surgery; The Polar World; Pompeii; The Pond; Ponies; The Potter's Palette; Prairie Dogs; Prayer; Prehistoric Life; The Press; The Primitive; The Pronghorn; Prophecies: What Can We Believe?

Notes toward the making
of a whole human being:

or, Deep Springs—being the incredible true story of twenty-five boys and their struggles to attain both bodies and souls at a small desert college in the American West (considered by some the best in the U.S.) for which young men at eighteen are plucked from the East and delivered to a campus surrounded by mountains, the size of Manhattan, closed off from the world by a series of cliffs, honor, dehydration, cattle guards, mountain lions, community censure, nearly fifty-three miles to the next human outpost, and the lure, at eighteen, of a world behind walls where boys can be boys, and (very often) are, for this college is also closed off to all girls, an experiment since October 1917 in fashioning citizens by Platonic means (by which is meant ideals; which means, of course, that young, bright, physically ripe boys, approximately aged eighteen to twenty-two, are trained under a curriculum of Heidegger and hay bales, St. Augustine and alfalfa, Locke and lassoing young calves to the ground, clipping their ears, branding their rears, cutting quickly into their one-year-old scrota, ripping out the cord connecting the two testes, removing them, rinsing them, and carrying them carefully to a bucket beside a grill where several hundred pairs are then broiled for a feast of what the boys have varyingly called

"Spring Poppers," "Rocky Mountain Oysters," and, even, "Swinging Beef") all of which has resulted in a gush of mass-media praise (e.g., *Chronicle of Higher Education,* 1987: "Welcome to Nirvana"; *Esquire,* 1992: ". . . such a world unto itself that it can't be explained but only intuitively grasped, like an epiphany"; The *New York Times,* 1993: ". . . at 3 o'clock one recent morning fifty miles north of Death Valley, seven young men, naked and illuminated by the moon, scrambled over mountain ranges made of sand . . . then climbed the dunes' highest peaks and began to slide down into the white nothingness seven hundred fifty feet below, feet first or head first, on their stomachs or on their backs . . . bellowing Broadway show tunes, discussing women, silently contemplating the stars"; *Smithsonian,* 1995: "I watched as A. was allowed a final say before the vote . . . a lanky, handsome dude, laid-back yet somehow immensely charismatic, a loner who projects terrific self-confidence . . . after which the student body then returned with its vote overwhelmingly in favor of A.'s request to keep a gun in his room"; or *People,* 1997: ". . . hard bodies . . . huge minds . . .") which in turn has resulted in an equally large gush of self-congratulatory writing by the boys about themselves (e.g., in the *Alumni Newsletter 1997,* "Introducing the New Fall Class": ". . . since his arrival N. has shaved his long blond locks and lifted innumerable hay bales during his term as Feed Man, proving himself truly a force to be reckoned with and thus earning the respect of his fellow students, as shown by his election to the position of Labor Commissioner . . . which any lesser man would surely use to overpower the democratic institutions of the Student Body and establish himself as a tyrant in the manner of the generals of ancient Rome . . . but like another famous Virginian, N. has done nothing of the sort, and is admirably executing the responsibilities vested in him . . . "; ". . . the name is deceptive . . . D. is not, in fact, the son of the Swedish war-god Ole"; " . . . B. has quickly distinguished himself as the pillar of democracy on campus with his eloquent tirades against tyrannical and consensus governments, self-indulgent experimentalism, and that which is contrary to freedom in general . . . as when his commanding grasp of conversational political theory, passion for Keynesian economics, and honed, cynical wit ran to a degree significant enough to draw blood during the grand potato harvest of Term One when an innocent bystander was wounded, superficially, during a violent brawl between B., liberty's spectacled advocate, and M., the brawny Marxist scholar from the wrong side of the iron curtain"; ". . . L. plays guitar and harmonica . . . he's in the middle of writing his first novel . . . he has the highest bench press of any member of the Student Body . . .") thus establishing at the school a hyper-conscious self-reflexive atmosphere best illustrated perhaps by Friday nights at the school, a night during which undergraduates elsewhere around America usually emigrate off campus to bars and parties and athletic events, yet which is spent at this desert campus at a weekly traditional gathering called "Student Body," a democratic meeting in the classical Greek tradition in which all students participate (for upon matriculation students sign the school's deed of trust, temporarily becoming the owners of this ranch, the alfalfa fields, desert as far as the eyes can see) regularly discussing in these meetings an itinerary of far-ranging import (such as which courses should be taught in upcoming terms; which professors should be hired, which professors fired; which new students from the applicant pool admitted; whether women should ever be allowed to attend; if the campus dog should be spayed; if B. should be kicked out; if L. should be censured; if S. can leave campus for three days to attend his grandmother's funeral; if C. should be forced to resume taking his antidepressants; whether the boarding house is being left too messy after midnight snack runs and, most importantly, what to think about this; whether Susan Sontag should be invited to campus in order to deliver the commencement address, and if not her then what about the guy who wrote *Lipstick Traces*) all of which are voted for not by ballots or raised hands but by finger-snap sounds rising secretly from the anonymity of each student's lap, behind their backs, beneath the cushions on the couches and lounges and chairs, making for what the reader will discover in the course of this study an interesting metaphorical dichotomy between what some call the "ego" and "superego," or, in other words, what is an illustration of the differences that exist between the phallocentric-frontiersmanship exhibited by the boys (such as in their long, long meetings; long, long hair; long, long sentences in papers and speeches, as if there were a fear in the desert like the fear at both ends of America since it started that if we were to pause to breathe, take a photo, send a postcard, set up camp for a spell in the middle of this great American periodic sentence westward, then we would lose our place on the trail, we would lose our captive audience waiting for a grand conclusion at the coast, the way Romans waited breathlessly for Cicero to complete his elaborate and long-winded sentences, even though Cicero knew himself that when his sentence finally ended then so would the Republic, as well as his life) and the simultaneous ironic sense that these boys are regressing into another part of themselves while they are at the school (one of whom, for example, lost a testicle in an accident; another of whom engaged in fellatio with a milk calf; another of whom single-handedly cut down the campus flagpole, "just because," then raised it up again; another of whom appeared on horseback in drag with lasso, hat, spurs, and dusters in order to greet the correspondent from *Outside* for a tour; the ones who run away; the 53 percent of whom never go on to marry; the one who returned to campus for alumni weekend and did not like what he saw, thus announcing suddenly that the last annual meeting of the Cigar Smokers' Circle would be gathering on the porch after lunch; and the one who reminded this author that sometimes a cigar is just that) like holes in a map that is used too much, opened and folded, worn slowly down, torn and then shredded, sinking continents along creases, draining whole seas, postponing America's great myth of frontier, as observed by the author, a former student and friend, assigned to tend the garden in this desert—is strange.

DOOR NO. SIX

Quigong: A Chinese Exercise for Fitness, Health, Longevity, Life.

Radium. Redeeming Love. Rhinos. Rockets. Rockets and Missiles. Rocks and Minerals.

Salvage, Sand, Sculpture, Seagulls, The Seasons, Seeds, Sharks, Sheep, The Ship: Or, the British Seaman's Marvelous Museum and Entertaining Companion, Skiing: A Method of Correct Skiing and Its Applications to Alpine Running, The Sky, Snails and Sound, Solitude, Speech, The Spider World, Sponges, Starfish, The Stereoscope, Stones, Swamps.

The Telescope Terns Terrariums Thai Art Thread A Gift of Textiles from the Collection of Elizabeth Gordon The Tropics The Turtle World Turkeys.

Unaka in Unicoi County.

The Vegetable World Victorian Engineering.

The Wasp's Nest Water Waterfowl A Week at Bath The West A Novel The West Indies Wild Ducks Wildlife With a Special Selection of Animals From Other Lands Nature Observed in 280 Pictures Wireless Telegraphy Explained in Simple Terms for the Non-Technical Reader The Woods and Desert at Night Woodchucks World Aviation The World Abroad Being Some Reminiscences of a Trip Around the World Illustrated with Numerous Remarkable Camera Pictures The World Between the Tides Comprising Man Quadrupeds Birds Fishes Trees Plants Mountains Caves Volcanoes Rivers Cities Remarkable Ruins Edifices Antiquities Bears Horses Shells Seas Land Fresh Water and the Many Secrets In-Between.

Collage History of Art, by Henry Darger

Pack: something with which to see. Bring trousers as well for the vegetation is thick. Sometimes storms, so a poncho would be smart. Also, war: in which case follow the instructions of your guide. A box lunch is provided. Do not drink the water. Please note the schedule of the moon's fall and rise as detailed on the back of your itinerary, enclosed. Memorize this. It will be your best friend. It will be on the test. It will be in your best interest to carry wrapped gifts for our hosts—men, women, children, parents, long-lost friends, sleek-winged beasts—but do not, under any circumstances, carry cash on your person. Cameras may be cumbersome but by all means sketch. Ready? Questions? Not now. Go!

HE COMMENCED THE LONG STRUGGLE not to express what he could see, but not to express the things he did not see, that is to say the things everybody is certain of seeing but which they do not really see.

SHE REMEMBERS IT WAS A SATURDAY but can't remember *day* or *night*. The window in Henry's room was covered with tinfoil and the wallpaper was hidden beneath several hundred faces. She remembers taking a step closer to see exactly whose: girls. Photographs, drawings, cartoons, and stills, from newspapers, magazines, dress patterns, lunch pails. She took a step back. All their eyes were *X*-ed. I didn't know if this was a joke or what, she says. Against the walls lay piles and stacks, bundles and bags, trunks and crates and a cage. I found things in there that I lost years ago, the landlady recalls as we walk through the room. Things that smelled rotten, things that looked rare. Henry's landlady found boxes full of icons from religions she'd never heard of, photographic negatives filed and cross-filed, mounds of wax crayons worn down to a nub. On a large metal folding table in the middle of the room was a collection of arms, legs, and heads drawn onto heavy pink butcher's paper. The tin ceiling had been painted black and the floor dusted with pencils. There was a chair with a blanket on it, another chair beside that. And against the far wall was a long and narrow bed, covered with what looked like brightly colored children's sheets. She looked closer: they were paintings. She stepped back: they were landscapes. Beneath the bed in eight neat stacks were the notebooks she had given Henry every year for Christmas. Closer: forty years' worth. Closer still: all filled. Closely reading some of them over the next few days, Henry's landlady realized that they were novels, memoirs, histories, prophecies—a hoard of 21,000 pages all typewritten and indexed. Over the next few years the paintings and writings would be visited by scholars, psychologists, and curators, all of whom agreed that the landlady's eighty-year-old tenant who had washed dishes for a living and never spoken a word to her—not of art, not of anything—had left behind the largest collection of outsider art ever created by an American.

HERE'S WHAT I KNOW: Born H. Joseph Darger on April 12, 1892, his father is a tailor, his mother a housewife, and together they lived in a small house at 350 Twenty-fourth Street, Chicago. He is the only child. Later that year, sometime in September, Henry is born to an unwed seamstress in the city of Cologne, Germany. The following year: Brazil. Henry's given South American name is Dargurius. 1896: due to complications during labor, Henry's mother and infant sister both die at the Alexian Brothers Hospital, Chicago. The infant is immediately given up for adoption. She comes home in a basket. Enjoys piano and dance. Henry himself is sent to an orphanage. He is sent to an asylum. He experiences a period of unrecorded years. 1896–1900: the Lincoln Asylum for Feeble Minded Children houses the nation's "most violently deformed and retarded patients under the age of seventeen," according to a 1901 House Committee Report on Children. Number of beds for 1,562: 900. Henry is there because his father is dead. Because his father is tired. Because Henry was caught setting a warehouse fire in which several hundred dollars worth of prized rabbits were killed. Why is Henry there? "Little Henry's heart is not in the right place," according to patient evaluation, 1905. 1906: "Masturbation." Henry runs away: 1908. Number of attempts preceding escape: eight. Employer number one: Alexian Brothers Hospital. Education: none. Apparent source of Henry's encyclopedic knowledge of the American Civil War as displayed to his coworkers in the hospital's gray wards: . Henry begins writing, in 1911, the story known to you as "The Realms of the Unreal." Full title: *The Story of the Vivian Girls, in What is Known as the*

Realms of the Unreal, of the Glandeco-Angelinian War Storm, Caused by the Child Slave Rebellion. Plot: good vs. evil. Fuller plot: war ravages the planet Abbiennia on which a good Christian child-nation is enslaved by haughty men, thus inspiring seven immortal, identical, curlicued blond sisters to rally the good children against the bad men until terrible bloodshed (number of men "killed" during battle: 63,821; number "mortally wounded": 63,973,868) persuades the men to surrender to the sisters and ultimately convert. Abbiennia's blue moon is Earth.

"HENRY ON THE STAIRS" IS A PHOTO you've probably seen. It depicts the artist as a lonely, scary old man. Unshaven, unwashed, unaware of why we've come to stare, he's been somewhere so sad for so long that his eyes, God help him, cannot look up. But earlier than this, in 1910, Henry makes a photograph at the Midway with a friend. He and the boy each pay eleven cents, then climb up a platform before a makeshift set. The object of the photograph, according to the backdrop, is for the young men to pretend that they are at a ball. The huge scrim sinks behind them toward a party. Above their two heads a chandelier is abloom. Henry's young friend sits cross-legged, hatless, staring us down. He's taken off his overcoat, rolled up his sleeves. He's about to reach out and take us for a spin, maybe even ask if we have a cousin for his friend. Henry, meanwhile, looks past the camera's lens. Not behind it, but beyond. Past the little machinery of make-believe surrounding him, off into the afternoon faces gathered round, the people standing by who are watching as they wait, eagerly anticipating their own turns at pretend. Henry, at this time, is new to "pretend." He's eighteen years old and has just escaped from an asylum. His expression, in this photograph, is one of pure shock—his eyes and mouth and whole face agog—as if he's caught the whole world in the midst of doing wrong.

THERE WAS A GARBAGE STRIKE, a mob war, a great, long Depression. There were things piling up on Chicago's streets as if the city had orphaned them. Henry could be seen on the sidewalks in the '30s pulling dolls out from trash heaps, tiny leather shoes, any magazine in which girls appeared in ads. He even tore the horsehair from an old chaise lounge. He took newspaper clippings of children lost in fires, rusty metal toys, spools of ribbon frayed, comic books, candy wrappers, stout pink bodies of Pepto Bismol bottles. Henry clipped a photograph of a little girl from the *Daily News.* The headline above it was just one word: *GONE!* According to Henry Darger, everything could be saved. He kept a list. It grew. Literature originated on clay desert rolls that itemized sheep, wheat, debt; that unraveled into praise for the wealthiest landowner, into laws and writs, into myths about chaotic pasts when nothing cohered, made no sense, hadn't ever heard of a thing called *list.* Beside the 15,000-paged, typed-and-single-spaced, hand-bound-and-illustrated list of Henry's world, there were 753 wound balls of twine and fishline and rubber bands and thread that were found in his apartment after Henry was dead. He searched for knotted string in the garbage heaps he scavenged, practiced untangling all of their kinks, tied the pieces together, rolled them into balls.

IN THEIR SLEEP, HENRY WROTE, "which lasted only a few hours without interruption, they had a long and beautiful dream. This was their dream. They had been put into a very large cell, where they wandered around for a very long while, when finally they grew very tired, and sat down on the hard stone floor, just ready to cry, when all at once, a dear child of unearthly beauty, appeared before them, and asked what was the trouble, and why they were about to cry, so they told the celestial child all about it, and she said, Never you mind, we will all take good care of you. Don't be afraid. There is a golden carriage waiting in the street for you. I'll take you to it, and then I'll go on ahead, and see that supper is ready."

ONE MUST HAVE A GOOD MEMORY to keep the promises one makes. Art, for example, originally emerged out of the need for good hunts, strong offspring, safe journeys through death. Art allowed the earliest humans to represent things they couldn't have, hoped to have, had too much of to carry. "Modeling," scholars call it, the fundamental element of which is the copy. Henry, who was classified retarded and never formally taught, knew as little about art as the earliest humans. Collage is the slowest route between two points.

ONE DAY HE HEARD A VOICE WONDERING, What if. She was sitting on a tuffet, eating curds and whey. Then along came a spider—which Henry erased.

HE WORE A LONG TRENCH COAT, grew a long beard, added small penises to every naked girl. I paint with my prick, Renoir once said. At first this is the most striking element in Henry Darger's art: that boys don't exist, and yet the girls all lack vaginas. No place of origin, no real womb. Where did Henry come from? In one painting there is an odalisque in recline in a garden. Flowers all around her are fecund and rotting, producing blooms so fast and so large that nobody bothers to pick them. Instead, the girls in the background, the foreground, all around the woman, play amidst the odalisque's seduction of the garden completely oblivious, as if her long stretch of mounds across the landscape were the very hills they run up and down. Long trains of girls with outstretched arms carry beach balls, giant strawberries, hats blown off their heads. Some of the girls carry nothing at all but whatever they can see in the distances ahead. Henry Darger's paintings burst like blooms from thin air. He never studied art—was never shown art—which is why Henry's girls all look like paper dolls. He cut them out of magazines, then glued them onto landscapes. So often repeated, their origins are moot. Yet where he wants to take his girls is the real question unfolding in all of our laps. Unfolding like a rhyme that Henry keeps repeating. Unrolling like syntax in the midst of translation. It is with my brush that I make love, is also a version of what Renoir said.

PROPHETS OF NATURE, WE TO THEM WILL SPEAK a lasting inspiration, sanctified by reason, blest by faith: what we have loved, others will love, and we will teach them how.

Cumulus, now. The blossoming, puffed, low-lying kind. They sweep across the landscape like girls having fun. In his paintings we can see precipitation—but only some. There is just enough for a rainbow. And over there, light drizzle. It falls so lightly, with so subtle a plop, that we look up to see it, hold our hands out to catch it . . . but then decide we like it, so why bother trying to prove it? In the distance is some lightning, calligraphy on hills. And above the mountain distances are blue skies embracing clouds in full view. If his paintings had windows we could point to what we feel. If Henry's paintings were a window, would we agree on what we feel? Am I the only one, for example, who sees Shirley Temple? Little Miss Muffet? The Campbell's Soup Kids? Henry Darger's paintings feel like something clogged in clouds: not childhood exactly, but the skies that hung above.

COULD THE FLAP OF A BUTTERFLY'S WINGS in Brazil set off a tornado in Texas?

WHEN YOU'RE ALL ALONE everything belongs to you. All the good and bad. Every yes and no. Whether to kill that little girl, or not. It was sometime in his late twenties, Henry tells us in his journal, when he lost the newspaper clipping of the girl from the *Daily News*. He prayed to God to return it, but God never did. Soon, war hung down around him from the towering piles of garbage that he had rescued from the streets. He hung his head over his notebook on the table and roared down at the girls who were playing in his trees. In some of his paintings: notice running. The black clouds hovering. Purple shade down. Yellow cracks severing the nano-strip of sky. An angled craze of fleeing girls is set against a phalanx marching. One soldier reaches and grabs an orphan by the throat. Her green eyes wobble, and then they bulge. One soldier spears an orphan in the spine. Her eyes pop out, replaced by an X. Eviscerations are happening at the feet of hills and trees. Of Henry, of God. The Coppertone baby has been left for dead, the Campbell's Soup Kids are all running in a pack, Little Miss Muffet is crying, naked, scared. As the children try to scatter the sky presses down, and the whole picture frame, likewise, spreads.

MILLIONS OF SOLDIERS ON BOTH SIDES howled at each other like demons, Henry wrote in volume seven of his novel *The Story of the Vivian Girls, in What is Known as the Realms of the Unreal, of the Glandeco-Angelinian War Storm, Caused by the Child Slave Rebellion,* "striking at each other, pouring a murderous fire at point-blank range, cutting, stabbing, hacking, thrusting, and slashing like wild savages bent on wholesale butchery, while amid all this was an indescribable tumult of bayonets adding to the riotous din, the Angelinian girls wavered in the furnace of fire, staggered, broke and ran, but undaunted they regathered again in hundreds of human waves, plunging again into the mighty inferno of fire and smoke, whole gray lines roaring like a trillion cannon blazing like hell and its damnation, the Angelinian girls wavered again, fell back, rallied, swarmed upon the first line of works only to go down in scores of hundreds of thousands, a fourth time beaten back, rallied, swept to the assault, reached the first line of works in the face of the murderous canister and gripped the torn and tottered and bleeding line with their dead piled in windows, only to again rally and rush to the assault like a whirlwind, the tempests of canister and musketry fire withering their many waves, a sixth time they rallied, sweeping within a hundred feet of the position, as far even as the second breastworks like a whirlwind of flaming flesh and steel pouring over the bodies of their dead and dying comrades in the face of a withering roar of artillery musketry that now seemed to stun even the heaven and the earth."

WHEN DID YOU FIRST NOTICE something missing in the world? Henry Darger died and was then brought to life. When his paintings were discovered they were "mounted," "framed," and "hung." They were "lit." Look at the painting of Henry's girls in a cave, huddled together beneath the red hard clay, and ask yourself why we bury what leaves. Stalagmites fang around them. The air is lacquered red. Now the soldiers who pursued the girls have stopped to picnic on a knoll instead. As long as the girls are out of sight, the girls are out of mind. Once there was a woman from the Smithsonian Institution who flew to Chicago to buy Henry's room. Here is a detail: she wanted all of Henry's paintings, wanted all of Henry's journals, wanted his novel that's so long no one has read it, the very walls around everything, the ceiling above everything, the floor beneath everything, and copyright control. She wanted her sound crew to fly up to Chicago, record several hundred hours of interviews with Henry's neighbors, and then loop their voices through his reconstructed room so museum-goers in Washington could walk through Henry's life. In the end, however, the deal fell through. Oh, said the woman, when she entered Henry's room—briefly seeing the Jesus shrine, the boarded window, the hundred some-odd drawings of little girls nude—then departed the same day for Washington. The girls in his paintings have coiled far below the seeded world. Past history, past art, into a vast cavern that's nearly dark, where their bodies are descending into the sinking red light from polka-dotted dresses, to silhouetted shapes, to gone from our eyes like an opened-up grave. Beginnings, Henry wrote, are hard. He remembered his father first telling him this when he dropped the boy off in the driveway of his new home, the Lincoln Asylum for Feeble Minded Children. Henry's young mother and unborn sister had just died during a labor that lasted twenty-three hours. Beginnings, Henry reasoned, don't even exist.

HENRY'S GIRLS—GRANTED—are already dead, but imagine in his paintings that they are living instead. Imagine, for example, how you would kill for art. In order to illustrate his great bloody war, Henry knew he somehow had to gather dead girls. But magazines in his day seldom published such illustrations. This, then, is how Henry first learned about color. Once cut out of magazines and pasted on the page, the girls were surrounded by washes singed with war: black shattered glass, blue melted steel, orange rusted barbs, smoke poisoned red. Henry filled in gaps as if the world would trip without him. Are girls in a wagon in the middle of a war going out to play, or are they going to their graves? Who is worthy to open the book and break the seals thereof?

Van Gogh used to swallow mouthfuls of dried paint. Miró starved himself. Dalí said he performed "autohypnotism" to create. Meanwhile, however, in French mental wards, Adam Christie sculpted with broken glass and nails; Martin Bigsby sewed lacey dolls' clothes from his skin; and when Aloise Carbaz lost her privileges to paint, she began to draw self-portraits with lily stamen instead. In March 1945, while passing by one day, Jean Dubuffet decided that art could happen anywhere if it could happen in sanatoria. Art, he wrote, could be spontaneous, unprocessed, full-blown *brut,* yet still recognizably artful if only we would look. He began that fall to search for it in mental hospitals, prison yards, and soup-kitchen lines, and by 1948 over 5,000 works by 200 artists were gathered in an exhibition he called "Compagnie de l'Art Brut." According to Freud's theory of recapitulation, the development of psychosis in an individual brain follows the evolution of the whole human race. God blew, Picasso said at the opening, and we were scattered.

NOW LET'S PLAY A GAME! When the girls who look like they are picking flowers bend, think to yourself that they are really lifting stones. When the girl mixing cake batter in a large bowl at her waist raises a spoon as if to stir, know that she holds a drumstick instead and is really in the midst of playing a snare. And when the forest animals gather in the clearing to play, be honest with yourself: they have come for the scraps of war. This is the game that Henry likes to play: a gray wash over everything familiar to make the seams around our memories fade. The trees blown bare in the gunfire are gray. The fence and its shadow—like a ladder on the river—gray. Blood streams out of everyone gray. As is the mud that's made beneath them. And the world that's stuck around them.

MUSEUMS ARE LIKE THIS ROOM. They're not arguments and answers, not stories with a meaning, not hallways linking galleries and adding up to plot. This is the place Henry lived in for forty years. A tour group files through the room and stares at nothing but the mess. Where did he sleep? they ask. Oh, there's the bed! The landlady lifts plastic sheets off the two chairs and bed, the large table and crayons, the four wheel-less tricycles in a corner, red. There are no more paintings in Henry Darger's room, but there is still a mess. There is still a stack of manuscripts that no one yet has read. Still a search for a patron who'll take this room off her hands. A Henry Darger original averages 85 grand. Once he is scattered around the world like crumbs, how will Henry Darger find his way back here?

DAY, IN 1913, WHEN HENRY WITNESSES a tornado destroy an entire Illinois town: Easter. When a handwritten draft of "The Realms" is completed: 1916. When Henry is drafted: 1917. When Henry is demobilized: 1918. "The Realms" is type-written by 1922. Number of single-spaced legal-sized pages: 15,145. Volumes: 9. Titles of other literary works of equal or greater length in the world: . Number of pages occu-pied in "The Realms" by a single quotation from *The Pilgrim's Progress*: 59. Number of accompanying watercolor illustra-tions: 318. Average painting's length: 12½ feet. Number of first-edition copies of Frank Baum *Oz* books: 7. Moves to one-room Webster Street apartment in fashionable Lincoln Park. 1945: registers for conscription. Income, before taxes, 1963: $1,216.32. Year Henry begins to write autobiography: 1966. Number of pages: approximately 5,000. Number of times in autobiography Henry Darger mentions he is an artist: none. Number of pages detailing Henry's dishwashing adventures: approximately 5,000. Number of times, per day, Henry attends mass: 4. Sometimes: 7. Years Henry chronicles the local weather forecasts: 13. How often do you do this: he does this everyday. When do you die: 1973. Number of washed and dried Pepto Bismol bottles discovered inside Henry's room as logged by the landlady on a clipboard she shows me: "several large black plastic bags full." Number of black bags filled with twine: 6. Number of broken eyeglasses, magazines, newspapers bundled up blocking the door; of bro-ken toys, sewing patterns, record players, crucifixes, men's shoes/ladies' shoes/children's shoes, plastic Jesus dashboard statues; typewriters, radios, ways to love a girl . . . How many bed linens, pillows, blankets do you have: for weeks on end I imagine Henry simply couldn't find his bed.

I'm sorry if I misled you into thinking this would be fun. That a paragraph could stand in for Henry Darger's room. That this essay could be a gallery you could walk through on your own, that you could get to know Henry on a Sunday afternoon. What I meant to say is that Henry never had any guests. I didn't mean to say *apartment,* but maybe *stanza* instead.

noun, singular, English: *poem*
noun, singular, French: *stance*
noun, singular, Italian: *room, chamber, stopping place*

CHILDREN USUALLY INTER THEIR PARENTS, Herodotus wrote in the earliest *History*, but war violates this natural order, and causes parents to inter their children. He is sitting there at his table with twelve feet of cave-black crayon covering his hands, trying to recall his father's face in their night-pitched kitchen after candles ran out, before the war worries of money crept up between them both, before poor little Henry got buried in the past. Henry was never taught about History in school, and so he never learned this word that's wrapped around him: *interred.* He looks over at the bed where the first five volumes of his own war lie bound. Does every life have a story? Why am I alone? He picks up volume one: eleven feet of paintings bound tightly together by glue and wire and cardboard and thread and can't remember for the life of him how this all began, nor why he even bothered, nor what should happen next. Kneeling on the floor he lifts with both hands the front cover up. Midway open the book scrapes plaster and photographs and crosses off the wall—then it jams against the ceiling. His room is too small.

THAT WHICH IS GROWS; that which *is not* becomes. If Henry had been diagnosed with schizophrenia in his lifetime, he most likely would have encountered Dr. Walter A. Freeman, the best-known American psycho-surgeon of the day, and pioneer of the ingenious "ice-pick lobotomy." Between 1942 and 1952 alone, over 5,000 lobotomies in the U.S. were performed—one-third of them by Dr. Freeman. "Much less intrusive than conventional surgery with a drill," Dr. Freeman once explained to *Time* magazine, "my technique, with an ice pick, enters the brain subtly by way of the eye socket." Already, *Time* reported in 1945, scores of patients have been saved by Dr. Freeman's technique. But Henry, in his paintings, depicts giant winged dragons called Blengins saving girls. Henry has known about Blengins all of his life. They are ferocious creatures, but they love little girls. And their sequined long tails hold a secret at the tip: when pierced by one in the breast, a child becomes immortal.

HENRY WRAPPED A GIRL in pink butcher's paper. He carried her outside, around the corner, and into the local drugstore. On the counter of the Photolab he unwrapped the little girl and asked the clerk to reproduce the drawing in five larger sizes and five smaller ones. Henry has realized, finally, that he can trace instead of cut. It is late in his life. He has hundreds of samples of girls in his collection. He knows that he will never be in search of friends again. From that moment on any girl whom Henry peels off his wall will be exactly the right girl for the space he needs to fill. He'll trace parts of one girl onto bits of others—arms from someone waving, legs from someone leaning, a dress from Cinderella, wings from birds instead—and thus render all the life happening outside his room, outside in the hallway, outside in the trash, outside where our lives are ready for his taking, moot. At the center of everything is a very small, black room; a heart, let's say, beating in the darkness.

A CROWD IS NOT COMPANY, and faces are but a gallery, and talk a tinkling cymbal, where there is no love.

WHEN HENRY DARGER DIED there was something blowing through the city. A breeze hard to distinguish between the *now* and the *then,* making Henry's life vanish into the rift therein. Trains, for example, arrived on time and didn't. Trees continued shading Chicago as they grew. The little girls on Henry's walls traded dolls, dated jocks, raised their children, peddled Avon, posed off and on for advertising photos, felt tired under the lights, blew bangs from their eyes. Upon Henry's death, no word blew through the city. No letters from pen pals were left behind when Henry died. No family heirlooms were discovered in Henry's room when he died. No neighbors held gatherings on their front stoops to share, in memorium, anecdotes of Henry's forty years on their hill. No one even knew that Henry lived on that hill. No obituary was written. No wake sat through. No grave. No history. No life. What to do? There is no history, Emerson said. Only biography. In the absence of information then, maybe biographers feel the need to fill their own lives sometimes into history's gaps—as if their own pasts could illustrate another's private world. But collage, as Henry wrote, is about collecting trash not dumping it. A biographer may feel the urge to cut from his life *divorce.* Paste it into the essay. Mean by that *the war.* He may sprinkle in some *casualties.* Stand back. Wait.

I SPEND A LAYOVER IN CHICAGO in Henry's small room. At noon his landlady brings a white crusty sandwich and a red bowl of soup. She asks how much longer I think I will be. I like the privacy of Henry's room with its foil-shaded window and black-painted ceiling and the eyes of his audience X-ed out with pencil. I like anything leadened. I like his paragraphs stacked, quotes amassed, blocks of prose boarding up the windows of his world. I'd like to stay a few more hours if that's alright, I say. She thinks I'm a reporter. How meticulous you're being. How thorough, she says. By the time dusk starts dropping I've filled a small notebook, read through a few journals, skimmed two volumes of the novel, know exactly what to write. It will be about Henry's wall of girls, about all their eyes. The little windows Henry boarded before leaving our world. Evening falls and there are no lamps to see by. I stand and gather my pack of notes. Zip up my coat. Lift my bag onto my back. Cars in the alley flip their headlights on. They come into the room through two tears in the foil. Driving up the ceiling, down the wall of girls. One pair of eyes is caught briefly in the headlights. She winks. Or blinks. Maybe I'm dreaming. Then another pair shines as a car sweeps by. Then more open, more shut. The opposite wall is sighing. I look closer: it's the lead. I stand back: it reflects. They're waking up. They're alive. The girls are waiting for Henry.

COLLAGE IS MADE UP OF THE PIECES in the box that are left after following all directions very carefully.

IT IS ALSO IN THE ACCIDENT on Interstate 89. In the shopping mall, in the family room, in the battlefield, in the stew. In the library, in the ruins, in the championship fight. In the rough draft, the rough cut, the rough-hewn night. In vaudeville, newspapers, attics, trains, the Internet, entropy, rap-song sampling. Collage occurred in the wondercabinets preceding all museums. It happened when scrolls of aphorisms unraveled into essay. When Henry walked past garbage and felt a jolt: *create!* Surely the heart must break before it can begin to feel.

DOOR NO. SEVEN

*The Wonders of Ye Deep the Wonders of the
Year 1716 the Wonders of Yellowstone and the
Grand Tetons Yorkshire Yogurt Your Senses*

*Zoos as Related to His Friends by Someone by
Maybe You Concerning Travels Memories Secrets Questions Searches Along the Way*

AND THERE WAS EVENING
AND THERE WAS MORNING

THE FIRST DAY

On my first day in Las Vegas, I looked for the light.

In a digitized photo from its gold-encased press pack, the brightest light in the world beams atop a hotel. The Luxor Hotel is heralded as "The Next Wonder of the World," a $400 million black-glass pyramid perched at the tip of the Las Vegas Strip, and broadcasting nightly this white beam into space. Closest to the airport—"See Our Sphinx From The Air!"—it is a tourist's first landmark, a pilot's sure beacon. At the same size as Egypt's ancient wonder at Giza, the Luxor boasts an atrium with a gift-shop replica of King Tutankhamen's tomb, a lounge called Nefertiti's, and an all-you-can-eat buffet at the Pyramid Café.

Sega debuts all its video games here; Motion Odyssey Movie Rides bump and grind guests through Egypt's history; at Accents, in the lobby, there is a cologne called Ramses; cartouches gleam eternally from the handrails, carpets, and every slot machine here—hieroglyph, *cherry;* hieroglyph, *lemon;* hieroglyph, *Ra, who gives life to wheat*—while we, upstairs, at 39 degrees, slant in our guest rooms unknowingly toward heaven.

Out of its apex the beam at Luxor soars ten miles into space. Bright, slim, straight. It reaches the clouds, the night, the vanishing point, but still does not disappear. At 40 billion candlepower, the Luxor's beam is the brightest, strongest, most visible light on earth. The FAA claims it can be seen from the air, 250 miles away, in L.A. And even NASA recently confirmed that while orbiting the Earth one could read a newspaper easily by its light. Up there, only two human structures on earth are visible: the Great Wall of China, and the light at the Luxor.

From where I sit in the back of the cab, the light looks like it's arched over us, a lure. The driver says he's new to the city.

"Still," he says, "I got this job real easy. All you gotta know is where you are in relation to Luxor."

Looking up at it for the first time on this night, my head out the window, the cab at a light, marquees humming on at the first hint of dusk, all I can think of is where the light goes, how far into forever, and if someone on the other side could be looking down it like a slide.

At first, I hardly notice the huge pyramid it issues from, nor the rest of the Strip, the traffic, the crook in my neck, the way heat lingers all around us—6 P.M. and still high in the nineties—from lit marquees, from guest-room windows, from headlights, streetlights, and all our hearts, gambling on fire tonight.

"My wife," says the driver, "she says it's like Jesus' eyes, you know? Wherever you go, it follows."

I check in. Take my key. Head to my room in the "inclinator." Below, a sparkling cavern drops, windowless, below-ground. According to the layout of ancient pyramids, the hotel's casino is Luxor's tomb. Cocktail waitresses wait by men at card tables, each woman wearing the same black wig, the same sarong, the long, long Hollywood eyes.

A Cleopatra counts out change. Her poker player tips in chips. The dealer rakes in all the bets, calls for bets, counts the bets. The slots chug out more change.

Everything glints accordingly.

Everything's still but chips.

Anything catching the light is gold.

Casino designers have long known what power light has on us. Walk into a casino built within the last decade and you will plunge, several feet, belowground. The natural light snuffed out. What illuminates these 100,000 square-foot spaces is the buzz, blink, and blur of tiny eye-level bulbs. Millions of them. The overhead lighting is indirect. The effect? Try to find your way quickly out of a casino. Try to maneuver over the thick, soft carpeting, the low-hung ceilings, the erratically rowed slot machines, through all these lights—orange, yellow, white—toward a tiny, singular, red *EXIT.*

We are awash in Las Vegas. Right now, through my window, the city drowns out everything in the desert. A few lights far away, from the old North End of town, blink soft echoes back. Ever since the new expansion of the South End of Vegas with its splashier, brighter, more expensive hotels, the North End's older downtown district has been in sharp decline: 2 million visitors per year, compared to the brighter South End's 29 million.

To compete, the eight largest hotels downtown have recently pooled $79 million to design and build "The Freemont Street Experience," an outdoor, 80-foot-high glass-and-steel cathedral vault that spans five blocks of sidewalk and street. At night, every hour, 2 million lightbulbs blast on and off, as lasers singe images of fighter jets, the Rat Pack, and dollars in the air.

They are fireworks that fall just feet out of reach. Some of us in the audience reach for them and stretch. All around me there are signs of new life downtown: families, couples, busloads of the elderly—all of us watching with our heads cocked up, all of us pointing to things shining up, all of our faces beneath bright stars.

Downtown was in decline, but now there are lights. "Come See What We've Done!" say the ads on the cabs, tempting us back to the new downtown attraction. I have seen its new lights.

I think they are good.

THE SECOND DAY

At a Malibu restaurant beside the sea, Joshua Thomas nods his head. Together we are making a list of light fetishes, and "Spiritual Encounters" tops it.

Joshua rattles off all the best-selling book titles from recent years that have dealt with near-death experiences, visions of gods, bright lights, and airiness. *Embraced by the Light, The Light Beyond, Light After Life, Lessons from the Light* . . .

"Why else would religions picture their gods as endless

sources of light?" Josh asks. "Everyone knows on some sub-conscious level that this is what gives us life, this is why we're here."

Josh gestures up toward the Malibu sun. I can almost glimpse his eyes behind shades.

Joshua Thomas is famous for having designed our bright-est light, but the beam atop the Luxor is only one of many he's made. Josh and his company—Brite-Nite Worldwide Light-Tech Solutions—have brought to light the Who's Farewell U.S. Tour, the International Powwow, the Hollywood Bowl, the Hollywood sign, the Los Angeles Olympics, and Walt Disney World, lighting up the amusement park on its Twen-tieth Anniversary with a seven-banded rainbow that arched a mile over "Main Street."

"But isn't bending light like that impossible?" I ask.

"All an illusion, my friend," Josh says, as he changes the subject to God.

"I figure I'm just reminding people of our roots," he says. "It used to be at night that we'd gather around campfires and worship the sun, praying that it would come back the next day. We did it for warmth, truth, and for protection against animals, but mostly, spiritually, we did it because it's the clos-est we could get to God. . . . These days, though, all we have are memories of that light, gleaming back at us in the stars."

Think of Prometheus. Zeus, as the story goes, became en-raged one night as he looked down on all of us and glimpsed our little fires. They flickered across the world like stars. Yet it is not the fact that Prometheus steals these flames which in-furiates Zeus. Rather, it is the sheer sight of all those "suns," private gods kindled by the hands of mere humans, which scares to death the King of Immortals.

I look up. There's a straw in Josh's mouth as he pauses to think. The wriggling of his fingers, gold rings, silver fork, the sun flickering off his hands like witchcraft.

When he grew up, Josh says, southern Indiana was full of "Protestants and wild weather." He'd go flying in a little piston plane through storms, he says, "and these clouds—these huge thunderheads on both sides of us—would leap across the sky and collide. Then there'd be this massive web of lightning all around us. But my dad and I would just go flying right through it!"

Was he scared?

No. The one thing the church taught him as a kid is that the world might end, eventually, but it will never end that way again.

"That's why light for me is so much more than a mere physics problem, or an aesthetic trick," he says. "For me, it's Truth. Light is, I mean. See, if you break light up into its component parts, then what you've really got is a rainbow, the spectrum. The Promise of the Old Testament. It's the symbol God sent Noah to tell him the world was safe again."

Ever since, Joshua Thomas has mastered light. Having majored in business and marketing in college, Josh is a quick wit, but he's remarkably unskillful on technical matters. He relies on a whole team of private electrical engineers to wrestle his sketches into reality.

"See, I'm a producer, man. A do-er," he says. "I get things done. Sometimes you don't have time to hear 'No.' You just gotta say 'Fuck it'—" he looks around, Malibu glances at us for an instant "—and just get on with your vision."

What struck me that day as I was speaking with Josh, and what has stayed with me since, is a vision of a man in love with the sky. Meeting him first at a gas station along the Pacific Coast Highway, I followed his black Chevy Blazer along the coast, into the mountains, and up toward the tiny cliffside restaurant he'd chosen for our lunch. On the way, I lost track of Josh's truck as it blazed up the coast, swerving between tourists and cruising local teens. Finally catching up with him, I wrote this down: *vanity plate, GRAVITY.*

He had stopped his truck in the middle of the highway. A surfer, feet in front of him, had just been struck down by another car.

The cops arrived.

Traffic jammed.

Josh got out of his car and called me over. "You're about to see something amazing," he said.

In moments, dozens of motorists, pedestrians, and golden-sunned bathers were in the middle of the street—heads cocked, shades on, ears alert for the copter that would fly over the mountains, circle the beach, and land smack in the middle of the Pacific Coast Highway.

From a hill on the right, a small, bearded, sunglassed man on a little red bike rode down the hill and stood beside us. It was Steven Spielberg.

Josh pointed and elbowed me. "Look at that," he said, giggling. "Beautiful, isn't it? It's an AL-80. Just look at that lateral descent!"

Yet what is even more striking about Joshua's sky than his almost single-minded obsession with imagining new ways to play with it, frame it, market it, and see it, is his consistent insistence on the necessity of it. At our table beneath the clouds, at the top of a small mountain, Josh dips into bowls of Mexican rice with his fingers, smacks his lips in Spanish, and lectures me about what is not just his *career* in light, but what he calls *the principal metaphor in all of Western thought*.

Dip.

Lick.

Smack.

Sky.

"Whether we're talking about cave art or Christianity, the Renaissance or this Luxor place, everyone's basically doing the same thing," Josh says. "And all of it's been going on since humans first opened their eyes."

Light = emotion, he says.

"We've known this for years. Hell, we've known it for centuries. Like in college, when I got into Zen meditation. You know how in Zen what you're supposedly going after is that so-called state of 'white light?' Well, all that really is is the pineal gland at work. You stimulate this little part of your brain and it secretes a fluid. It creates the sensation of being washed in light. Music does this, too. Architecture. Food. You name it. It's what we might call 'inspiration' in another context. And that's the great thing about all of this: that light literally is inspiration. It's hardwired into us. Biological. Just think of someone going into a cathedral in Byzantium. Think of the stained glass, the gold furnishings, the thickness of the air! No buildings in the world were more magical at the time. The Church had the money, the technology, and some mysterious other power that allowed them to actually change the color of the air. Think about that! Think about how manipulative that was back then. We humans lived hundreds of thousands of years without artificial light. So we have to imagine someone living in pre-Edison days—living in darkness, living in fear—then suddenly some guy comes along with a burning cross, let's say, to brighten things. Well, in a pitch-black village this is the best thing going! It's warm because it's fire, it's inviting because it's a cross, and hell—it's spectacle! Don't you think people would want to follow that guy?"

Now Josh is excited. He jabs out points in the air with spicy fries.

As he talks, shadowy memories come to new light. All the glares outside my bedrooms, the woodstove at my grandmother's, a first kiss, sunburns, Mother's search for God . . .

Yet, when I try to grab onto Joshua's words, his enthusiasm, or even just his eyes, there are still only adjectives—only *brightest, resplendent, shimmering, bold.* Only *the principal metaphor in all of Western thought.*

There is nothing to touch, to pick apart, to know. Where are the natural philosophers who invented light, that tangible ether? Where, Aristotle, is your visual cone, the lines you sketched out like antennae from the eyes, like a snare to catch light and feed it into our brains? Where is the light that spawned the Renaissance? And where does it go after flitting off our screens?

As a child, I remember looking at a photograph pulled out

of my grandfather's deep wooden war chest. In this picture was a circle of 360 distinct pillars of white light, each beside a beer barrel, each lined around a field. All of them were buttressing the night up above. Looking down at it beside me in his house, my grandfather said quietly, "This is why I joined the war."

Now I know that the image is of one of Hitler's famous Nuremberg rallies. There are, perhaps, a million people in the photograph, and every one of them is bright with hopeful eyes.

The entire spectacle was designed for Hitler by Albert Speer, the erstwhile set designer who helped prod a nation, and later a world, into war. His pillars of light have become so famous that no great opera can now be performed without them, no rock concert starts, no Hollywood premiere is premiered without first aiming his lights at the sky, grazing the darkness for an evil that we all hope dare not come. In fact, the searchlights that we use today are the same kind that Speer used at his Nuremberg rallies. And they are the same kind that crown the Luxor.

The impact of such lights is so potent that Speer's style is now known in lighting textbooks as the "Nuremberg Effect." What is its power?

I suggest, "A phallic symbol?"

"No," Josh says. "Think bigger than that. Think of the lighthouse at Pharos firing out to lost ships. Think of the Statue of Liberty first seen from Ellis Island. Think of symbolism, yes, but think too about the desperation that's inherent in our actions as humans when we make these things, let alone when we look at them and cry."

Maybe it's because Las Vegas is the brightest city on earth that we feel at ease tempting ourselves there. There is something about overstimulating light that encourages risk: to spend more money than we really have; to eat more, drink more, party more, fuck more—all in the face of Lucifer. Deep below sea level, near to his lair. It is this fallen dark spirit— whose name ironically translates into "Angel of Light"— whom we invite onto our laps for good luck as we spin the wheel, hurl the dice, look far up into night stars for advice, our last chip trembling on the table.

Elsewhere, there are other grand plans in the works for casting lights in the sky. Within the first few years of this new century, for example, a company called Space Marketing Incorporated plans to launch mile-wide display satellites into space—mylar billboards that will look as big as the sun and bear the logo or slogan or even the face of anyone who will be able to afford the few million dollars each ad will cost.

There's also news of a "new moon," as Russian scientists have called it—650 feet across and hovering above Siberia, designed to reflect light to those who spend months in darkness: to the villagers, the loggers, the miners, the banished.

And even Washington, it seems, has big plans for light, granting $40 million so far to the University of Alaska in order to test strategies for harnessing "those million amps at waste in the sky," those ghosts of the North called Aurora Borealis.

Meanwhile, outside, on the edge of the sea, the horizon is swallowing the rest of the day. Malibu is riding its last wave in. The cliff face crumbles into night.

I want to ask Josh about all these other lights, about whether he feels guilty for piloting a trend that could end up ruining the very sky he's in love with.

I look up at him through the dimming air as a thick pall of firmament falls over everything, and as he, quietly, looks out and says—to no one in particular, to no one in the world— "Nice blue."

THE THIRD DAY

A little warmth, a little light. Afraid of the light, all of us. Armour of light. A-roving by light. Black as if bereaved of light. Carrying you into fields of light. Certain Slant of light. Children of the light. Cold light and hot shade. Come on baby light my fire. Common as light is love. Consider how light is spent. Danced by the light of the moon. Darkness and light alike to thee. Dawn's early light. Dear as light and life. Dim religious light. Everlasting light. Excess of light. Existence is a brief crack of light. Faintly muddy light. Flash of light cut across the sky. Forward the Light Brigade. Freedom's holy light. From grave to light. Garmented in light. Gates of light. Gatsby believed in the green light. Gives a lovely light. God Appears and God is light. God is light. God shows sufficient light. God's first creature was light. Gone into a world of light. Guide by the light of reason. Heaven's light forever shines. Hesperus entreats thy light. I am the light of the world. I came into a place void of all light. If light in thee be darkness. If once we lose this light. It giveth light unto all.

Law not a light to see by. Lead me from darkness to light. Let the big light in. Let there be light. Let your light shine. Light at the end of the tunnel. Light of an oncoming train. Light of setting suns. Light of the body. Light of the world. Light of thy sword. Lift up the light of thy countenance. Little drops of light. Live and love in God's light. Live out thy life as light. Lolita, light of my life. Energy equals mass times the speed of light squared. Men of inward light. Neither joy nor love nor light. Noose of light. Not light, but rather darkness visible. People have seen a great light. Power and light. Purple light of love. Put out the light. Rage against the dying of the light. Something of angelic light. Stand in your own light. Strike Sultan's Turret with light. The first light of evening. The light that lies in a woman's eyes. The Lord is my light. Those that rebel against the light. Thousand points of light. Thy light is come. Time's glory brings truth to light. To whom God assigns no light. Truth will come to light. Two thousand light-years from home. Unveiled her peerless light. Walk while ye have light. We shall need no other light. What light through yonder window breaks. When our brief light has set.

THE FOURTH DAY

On the fourth day I find myself in the Las Vegas branch of the Nevada Sleep Center, 5 P.M. With me are Mary, Freddy, Shauna, and Wendy, plus two men who are hooked up to brain-wave machines and sleeping in private guest rooms as we watch them on green screens.

One of the men has come to the clinic because he is narcoleptic, a condition which will be first diagnosed tonight. The other man is here because his wife, he says, is tired of trying to fall asleep to the sound of his snoring. Both men have come here, to this clinic in particular, because it is arguably the best among the seven in Las Vegas, because it is one of the oldest in the country, and because it is run by a woman who was described to me once as "the grandmother of sleep"—Roxanne Melt. I myself have come to the Nevada Sleep Center because I saw its bright sign on my first night in town. I was driving down the narrow streets that run parallel to the Vegas boulevards—the tiny byways that are intended only for locals—and noticed all along them sleep-clinic signs, sleep-clinic billboards, sleep-clinic ads in the tabloid weeklies; posters, broadsides, fliers stuck to cars, fliers stapled to trees with their phone tabs ripped off. Passing by the clinics, I saw their windows all lit, their parking lots full, all their marquees as bright in the middle of the night as any casino's a coin toss away.

The clinic inside is entirely windowless. It has a shallow cathedral ceiling above its core reception room, and two desks underneath it that serve as monitoring stations. Around the perimeter of the clinic are more windowless rooms: offices for Roxanne and her two sleep partners, a bathroom, a laundry room, a medical-supply closet, and two guest bedrooms for two patients per night. Every room and every inch of wall is windowless. The two bedrooms are designed to be "very homey and comfortable, something like a hotel room," the clinic pamphlet explains. In each of the guest rooms is a bed, an easy chair, ceramic lamps, potted plants, and a wicker armoire on which a TV and VCR will play a film for the patients, "While You Are Here." Through the wicker's lattice patches are two small, black cameras that are aimed inconspicuously at both of the beds.

"It's for liability," Freddy says, showing me around. "You know, so we can see them, keep track. If someone's sleepwalking, for example, and bumping into everything and hurting themselves, then we can go in and help them back into bed."

"Tell him about the Candy Guy," Wendy says, walking by us while Freddy's giving me a tour.

"Well, yeah. It's good for that, too," Freddy continues. "Last night there was this guy in here getting tested—sleeping, we thought. All of a sudden, though, at like three in the morning, his EEG machine starts going crazy. I mean, just off the chart! We were freaking! We thought maybe the guy was having a stroke or something. But, hold on! I happen to look up at the monitor and I see him there sitting up in his bed. In complete, pitch darkness! Just sitting there, eating jelly beans!"

"How'd he get jelly beans?" I ask.

"In his sock," Wendy says. "The guy snuck them in his sock!"

"As if we weren't going to be able to see this," Freddy says. "I mean, come on! It screwed up a whole night's worth of research. So we kicked him out."

Tonight's two patients arrive by 8 P.M. and each start immediately unpacking in their rooms. I watch them on the monitors watch TV alone, trying to replicate a normal evening at home. I watch them undress. Watch one of them moisturize, brush his teeth, gargle. I watch as the three female technicians enter the rooms to shave the men's legs, shave the men's chests, shave the men's chins, and then wash the shaved parts. Then they attach with grey putty seventeen large electrodes that will monitor the men throughout the night's tests.

Meanwhile, Freddy's in the other room testing the machines.

"Okay," he yells from his monitoring station into one of the rooms. "Smile!"

The patient smiles. A little flurry of crests scribbles onto the test page.

"Okay. Now raise your left leg!"

He raises his left leg: canyons, then crests.

"Now look to the right!"

"Look to the left!"

"Look down at the bed!"

"Look up at the ceiling!"

"Furrow your brow like you're getting angry with someone!"

"Good. Breathe!"

Flurries, buttes, squibbles. Lights out.

It is 10:00 P.M. By 10:15 both men are asleep.

There are an estimated 100 million Americans with some sort of sleep disorder at any given time, which is why, according to the National Sleep Foundation, Americans spent an estimated $13.9 billion on sleep treatments in 1999. There are 84 different recognized sleep disorders from which we can suffer, but still roughly 80 percent of Americans have no idea they're afflicted. The most common sleep illnesses are narcolepsy, insomnia, nightmares, sleepwalking, sleep talking, teeth grinding, a fear of the dark, a fear of the light, lazy-leg syndrome, night-shift work syndrome, rhythmic-movement disorder, snoring, and jet lag. The American Sleep Disorders Association, a national advocate for sleep research, is so serious about sleep that it has been compiling an ongoing list of disasters throughout human history that could have been prevented if only those involved had been getting enough rest. Among the most recently listed culprits are those involved in the Seven Mile Island leak, the Challenger explosion, and Exxon's spill at Valdez. "If only they had been following a proper sleep schedule . . . ," the American Sleep Disorders Association reports.

Indeed, as researchers say, personal sleep hygiene can determine life or death. This is because our sleeping patterns directly affect our circadian rhythms, the biological clocks that we all have inside us. They can make us drowsy, peppy, angry, or sad, and course through our bodies in sync with our electrical, chemical, and emotional lives.

Circadian rhythms influence sleepiness, wakefulness, hormonal changes, even body temperature. No one knows yet for sure how or why these rhythms work, but researchers do know that they have something to do with light. Immediately behind our eyes runs a pathway of nuclei, and it is this thin cord of light-sensitive equipment that connects directly to the brain, dictating what beats our lives will make.

For example, even though my four hosts are all trained sleep specialists, when the lights in the clinic go out at 10:00 P.M., each of them falls silent, almost dazed without light.

There are now only a few lamps on for those working at desks. A gooseneck is swung close to the monitors on the wall. The front door is propped open, but no one steps outside. Freddy, Mary, Shauna, and Wendy are required to stay up until morning, straight through the night, until the two patients wake up, shower, dress, and then leave. But as mundane as this sounds, it is actually very difficult. Just watching them trying to stay awake is itself difficult. They can't play board games, can't talk on the phone, can't read magazines. All they can do is wait. Watch. Awake.

"What will you do after this?" I whisper.

"After what?" someone asks.

"What do you do when you leave here, I mean?"

None of the technicians answers "sleep." Instead, the four of them answer with a barrage of lists of errands they need to tend to in the light: favors for friends, baby-sitting, second jobs, second lives. Shauna even says she goes to school during the day, five times a week, in order to earn her own degree in sleep therapy.

"Wow," I say. "Kind of ironic, don't you think?"

She looks at me, red-eyed, then turns away.

Suddenly a beeping comes sirening out of a machine on the wall. It's the narcoleptic man's EEG. Once again the patient has lapsed into REM sleep—a brief, deep sleep during which our eyes move rapidly, and which usually is suggestive of the occurrence of dreams.

The crew hustles over to the printout and looks.

"Whoa!" they all shout.

Then, "Shhh!" with a giggle.

The four of them watch the printout the way some may watch a horse race, a ball game, an action flick with flurries of pyrotechnic tricks—cheering it on, guessing what's next, generally giddy with its fast action.

I walk over. The squiggles are now making mountains and gorges, not just small unconscious crests from random leg twitches in the middle of the night. The printouts are forming bold, towering, distinct peaks from each eye—one jigging left, one jagging right—each printing out so dramatically, so fast, and so close to one another that the crests actually scratch out a thin isthmus across the page. Compared to the snoring man's rippleless chart, the narcoleptic's printout is that of a mountaineer, a white-water rafter, a Lewis and Clark adventurer into the dark West of our dreams.

Or so I imagine. In reality, the narcoleptic man could be dreaming about gardening, walking, or even just sleeping. The ferocity of his REM printout doesn't necessarily correlate to his actual dreams. All it means is that wherever the narcoleptic man is in his sleep, he is there with practically the same conscious intensity he has when he's awake. Thus the four technicians diagnose him before the night is up with a severe case of narcolepsy. Case closed.

"Oh, I am so jealous!" Mary says, walking from the printout to the coffeepot again.

"Jealous?" Wendy says. "Jealous of what? This guy's sick!"

"I just want to sleep!" Mary moans, throwing back her head, rolling back her eyes.

Outside, a siren. Then wind whorling in. Someone switches a computer on and the lights briefly dim.

Generally, among humans, sleeping at night has been more desirable than sleeping at any other time. When we roamed prairies, deserts, and savannahs in our past, the impulse to sleep at dusk was natural, if not also smart. Humans, biologically speaking, are not well equipped for nighttime activities: our body temperatures drop, our eyesight fails, and creatures eons more nocturnally evolved come out to prowl for prey. We hide in our sleep. In our past, it was a refuge in which to pass the lonely, spook-filled nights as the shadows and their henchmen crept slowly by.

But when we speak as humans of the beginnings of life, we first recall the depths of a dark primal night, what is called a "dark chaos" in ancient Greek literature, a "black void" in Egypt, "endless caves" in China, "gloomy seas" in Phoenicia. The very first act of creation, after all—in any myth, at any time, among the powerful, the weak, the primitive or advanced—is the making of light to drive darkness away. With it go Grendel from Beowulf, Hecate from Rome, the Bogglemann from Germany, the Headless Trunk from Scotland, the Black Annus, the Night Hag, all Vampires, Werewolves, Liliths, Zombies, Abbey Lubbers, Banshees, Draculas, Boggarts. Whatever the night scares may be called in our minds, in our imaginations the darkness lets loose a host of beasts whose aim is to corrupt our very souls: the "nightmare" in England, the "cauchemar" in France, the "mahr" in Germany, the "mora" in Lithuania, each of them deriving from the Anglo-Saxon *mara*, meaning, simply, "crusher."

Now, in my hotel, after watching the snoring man wake up and drive off to work, after helping rouse the narcoleptic man and send him off in a cab, I am sitting up in bed at 9 A.M., trying to read myself to sleep. Edward Topsell, the seventeenth-century poet, is known primarily as one of the earliest encyclopedists. But in sleep circles he is legendary for spending many nights awake. Legend has it that he never slept more than a few minutes each night. Many believe that because of this he was obsessed—and some say cursed—by monsters and beasts and half-human freaks, and the mysterious lands from which each of them came. He wrote, through three years' worth of nights, the very first encyclopedia of impending evils in the dark.

I'd ordered the book through my library thinking the title was funny, that Topsell's "monsters," as he described them, were just strange animals from the New World, that the "mysterious lands" he warned of were just rare pockets of the Old. "A History of Foure-Footed Beastes," is what he called his collection, and I imagine Topsell's intentions were purely academic as he began, encyclopedic in the safest, most blandly scholastic sense. Yet as the breadth of the night unraveled itself around him through the years, as the catalogue of quadrupeds cornered him between bookends—eyes flashing, teeth glinting, sentences in packs hiding beneath the shadows—his encyclopedia grew to an unwieldy size, and Topsell began inventing new species to fend off his fears, describing familiar animals as "cursed," "bewitched," "woed," as his title likewise extended beyond the reason of his grasp, whipping wildly in the dark, snapping candlelight out: *A History of Foure-Footed Beastes: Describing the True and Lively Figure of Each, with a Discourse of Their Severall Names, Conditions, Kindes, Countries of Their Breed, Their Hate for Mankinde, and the Curious Work of God in Their Creation, Preservation and Hopeful Destruction, Necessary for All Divines and Students Because the Story of Every Beaste is Amplified with Narratives out of Scriptures, Phylosophers, Physitions, and Poets, Wherein Are Declared Divers Hyeroliphiks, Emblems, Epigrams, and Other Sad Histories, Collected Out of All Other Writers to this Day, for the Survival of Mankinde, and With Humble Warnings Hence.*

THE FIFTH DAY

Afraid to go home in the dark. All night in the dark. And his dark secret love. At one stride comes the dark. Between dark and daylight. Blanket of the dark. Chromis did not save himself from dark death. Come to dark and lament. Dark and lonely hiding place. Dark and stormy night. Dark as Erebus. Dark as the world of man. Dark, backward and abysm of time. Dark blue ocean roll. Dark care sits enthroned. Dark cloud at the house's door. Dark, cold and empty desolation. Dark, dark amid blaze. Dark, dark spaces. Dark dove with flickering tongue. Dark echoed with outlandish orders. Dark hawks hear us. Dark horse. Dark mother always gliding near. Dark night of the soul. Dark unfathomed caves. Dull dark soundless day. Ever-during dark. Everyone is a moon and has a dark side. Fate sits on the dark battlements. Fear death as children fear the dark. Fell of dark, not day. Great leap in the dark. Hunt it in the dark. In the dark and silent grave. Iron New England dark. Irrecoverably dark. Let the dark come upon you. Life is one long struggle in the dark. Narrowing dark hours. Night is dark. Night of dark intent. Not dark days, great days. Old fantastical duke of dark corners. Raging in the dark. Dark rebellious brows. Some days dark and dreary. Soul's dark cottage. The sun to me is dark. The wall between us and dark. The violets are dark too. Then it is dark. They all go into the dark. Ways that are dark. We are for the dark. We work in the dark. What if Amyntas is dark. What in me is dark illumined. Who art dark as night. Woods are lovely, dark and deep.

THE SIXTH DAY

"My other car's a Maserati," Roxanne Melt says as we hop up into her monstrous green truck on the way to our lunch on my sixth day in town.

"Yeah, right!" I say.

"No, I mean it," she says. "I got it last year. I don't drive it around downtown because . . . well, what's the point? There's always traffic downtown. You can't *drive.*"

"Wait. You really have a Maserati?" I ask.

"Yes, I really do," she says.

"Damn!" I say. "How sleepy are people in this town?"

Roxanne laughs. "Well," she says, "it is 'the city that never sleeps!'"

"Actually," I say, "I think that's New York."

"Trust me," Roxanne says. "It's Las Vegas."

When we arrive at a tiny six-tabled Thai dive we are immediately greeted by the host jumping and screaming.

"Ro-ahhn! Ro-ahhn!" he says.

Roxanne screams back at him, waving her bangled, tanned arms in the air.

She is tall, blond, big-boned, and action-packed. She is somewhere in her sixties—although I never learned for sure—and today is wearing a pair of skin-tight black pants and a tight fur-cuffed blouse with a rhinestone zipper that is pulled halfway down.

She is also, undoubtedly, one of the most talented practicing sleep therapists in America.

"I'm from Alberta," she says. "That's where I did my medical training as a lass, so being down here where there's always sunshine has definitely had a big impact on me."

"How so?" I ask.

"Well, I've noticed I'm much happier now. I'm even 'bubbly,' people say. I exercise more, I laugh more, I enjoy going to work more, and so I make a lot more money!"

She giggles.

"There's a much better climate down here obviously," she says. "But, more importantly, there's more *sunshine*. We're in the desert, remember. So: no rain. No rain: no clouds."

"I don't get it."

"Let me make this clear: I'm happier because of the light," she says. "It's *all* about light, honey. Remember that."

In Roxanne's world, even though darkness prevails, her career has thrived more than any other sleep specialist's precisely because of her experiments with light.

"With light?" I ask.

"Okay," Roxanne says, pulling her huge, bleached, weather

vane of hair into a tight, tall, northerly bauble on her head that starts jiggling as she closes her menu and begins:

"Have you ever noticed over there in New England that every year when winter comes you get really, really mopey?" she asks. "Have you noticed that? Maybe you start gaining weight, or you sleep too much, or maybe you even have trouble sleeping in the winter. I mean, you've heard of the 'winter blues,' right? Well, that's a real thing, honey. There's this condition called Seasonal Affective Disorder, and it's more common in the winter than it is in the summer. When people have it they feel lethargic, or they get fat, or they're always in bed, or they don't go out with their friends to the movies, and so on and so on. It's almost a cliché, right? It sounds like a lot of us. Well, we're not all crazy! A couple years ago we started figuring out that people get this way not because it's cold outside in the winter, but because there's less light in the winter. We don't know how yet, exactly, but light affects our brains' neurotransmitters. And it's our neurotransmitters that control our moods."

Pause. Breath.

"My point here is that this isn't psychology that we're dealing with. It's biology. It has to do with chemistry, not society, not with how your parents raised you or the mean thing your lover said to you. When patients are treated with light it makes them feel better because it helps them sleep better. And it helps them sleep better because with the right dosage of light you can trick their brains into thinking that it's brighter outside, and this kicks their circadian rhythms into gear. Now you know about circadian rhythms, right?"

In 1979 Norman Rosenthal, a psychiatrist at the National Institute of Mental Health, started experimenting with patients who were suffering from depression. Once a day he sat them in front of a huge metal box out of which emitted large "dosages" of white light. Over time the doctor raised the dosages of light until he finally noticed improved mood changes in his patients. What his experiments seemed to suggest is that when exposed for two or more hours at a time to a dose of light roughly 10,000 lux—approximately twenty times as bright as office halogen lights—patients showed an increased level of energy, a decrease in anxiety, lower weight gains, and, most importantly, more regular sleep patterns. Their circadian rhythms were kicked back into gear, in other words. In general, what has panned out from Dr. Rosenthal's experiments is that people who sleep better lead healthier lives—psychologically, physically, socially, even financially.

"There are certain hormones that our brains release while we're sleeping," Roxanne says. "Good hormones, important hormones. We know that when infants are sleeping there are enormous amounts of hormones released, even more so than in adults. This is because they're growing, of course. So, unfortunately, children who don't sleep well don't end up developing mentally or physically."

Outside, huge clouds roll off the sun. Then roll back on. Out of the window beside our table Roxanne stares, pausing, sunglasses on. Sunglasses off.

"What was I saying?" Roxanne asks. "Oh. Right. Kids. My god! Do you know they're starting to build schools without windows now? It's the newest thing. They say it's going to cut down on daydreaming during class. Do you believe that? All they have to do is look at juvenile delinquents to figure out that's a bad idea. You drive down the street at 3 A.M. and lo and behold, there they are, hanging out, in the middle of the night! Do you think these kids are up the next morning at dawn, ready for school? They're probably sleeping through half the day. Where are they getting their sun, all the light that they need?"

"I bet jails are the same way," I add. "I mean, they're pretty dark, right? And people don't seem to be happy in them."

"Okay, good. Now you're thinking. You know, there was this study of two little girls once. Twins. They were six years old. One of them was brilliant—outgoing, did well in school, popular, and she slept really well, too. Her sister, however— her sister had sleep apnea. She wore glasses, couldn't speak well, her motor skills were shot, and her grades were suffering horribly. But as soon as doctors figured out that she wasn't sleeping and corrected her apnea, her growth suddenly improved, her coordination was corrected, and the grades shot up dramatically. Her eyesight couldn't be changed, of course, and there's probably some permanent brain damage that she suffered, but she definitely is better off now because of the changes they made in her sleep."

Our food arrives. Racks full of spices. A phone call for Roxanne. Two Thai ginger beers fizzy and overflowing.

"So have you been there?" I ask.

"Where?" she asks.

"Thailand."

"Nope. And never will," she says.

"Why?"

"It's too tropical," she says. "The desert light is one thing, but down there I think I would be too stimulated."

"Too stimulated?"

"Well, how far have you traveled?" Roxanne asks. "How many different kinds of light have you experienced? Recently I've been wondering what would happen if we were to look at the geography of a culture and its effects on how that culture developed. In terms of climate, I mean. I bet we could find out some pretty interesting stuff about who those people are based primarily on how much light they're exposed to."

"How much sleep they're getting, in other words," I say.

"Yes. Or at least what kind of sleep. For example, take me. I'm from Canada. When I first came down here I thought you people were all crazy. I think most Canadians would agree. Americans are very aggressive people, you know. Why? Well, you live in a lot more sunlight for longer periods of time than we do. On the other hand, look at the Inuit. They're practically still living in the dark ages, and I would bet that a lot of that is due to their climate. But the Maya, in Central America, for example, had one of the most scientifically advanced civilizations on earth."

Sip of beer.

"Or, for example, take the Middle East versus Sweden," she says. "Eskimos versus Aborigines. Why do we call a place like Hawaii paradise and a place like Siberia . . . well, Siberia? Light improves our sleep patterns, and it thus improves our lives."

Just before I came west I found a brochure in the mail

from a lamp company called Microsun. "Get the natural light that people crave all year long," the cover read. It's "a technological breakthrough inspired by the sun," exclaimed a caption inside; for $500 per lamp the "power of the sun can be in your hands." The company was commissioned by the Library of Congress to redesign all of the reading lamps in the Great Hall in D.C. Now, "with special features like our sunrise start-up," the brochure claimed, "the rest of us can enjoy the natural feeling of the sun in our very own homes." "It's 7:30 P.M., mid-November, and it's raining," a woman in a photograph explains beneath one of the lamps. "I've never been happier." The cat in her lap smiles, too.

"I bet admissions to mental hospitals rise in the winter," Roxanne adds. "I bet murders rise. Suicides. Lots of things. I remember as a medical student I was assigned to a mental hospital in Alberta. For part of our training we had to observe mental patients over a 24-hour period. One full day, without any sleeping. We had to write down everything that they did in that period—every time they ate, went to the bathroom, bathed, played, read, whatever. After a while, though, I started noticing that a few of the patients never seemed to sleep during my watch. I mean, I would go back over my notes from monitoring these patients and there just wasn't any sleeping going on. So then I'd come back a few days later and make a point of looking over other students' observations of the same patients, and there would still be no indication that these patients were sleeping. At *all!* I'm not kidding about this. And keep in mind that these patients were on huge amounts of drugs! Now, come on, you don't think that we could dramatically help these people by at least starting to address the issue of sleep in these hospitals?"

Clouds pass. Her hair's down. Sun's falling everywhere.

"By the way," Roxanne continues, "they tell me you saw a patient a few nights ago who slept really heavily. Now, before you start misdiagnosing narcolepsy in your head, I have to correct what they told you because I don't think he's narcoleptic. I met him this morning. The guy's depressed, that's the problem. I don't know exactly what the cause is, but I know what part of the problem is: too much sleep, too much dark. Depression, it's true, is a chemical imbalance. But it's also a sensory imblance. It causes us to shut ourselves off from the rest of the world. We pull the shades down, stay under the covers, fold into a fetal position. It's a way of isolating ourselves, shutting ourselves off from all sensory stimuli. I mean, here we were, in the sunniest place in America, Las Vegas, Nevada, and this guy is covering his head with his hands as I'm walking him out to the cab! Darkness makes us feel isolated, and sometimes that darkness is something we seek out. But sometimes it's something we need help getting out of."

After lunch, Roxanne drives me back to the Luxor, and with darkness on my mind I finally notice something I'd previously ignored. It is lunch time, or just past, 3 P.M. and still bright, and yet every hotel we pass has already turned on its lights. Every marquee, spotlight, streetlamp, billboard, all neon outlining every architectural flair—all of it is powered and straining hard against the sun.

Why so early?

Dusk, in this town, passes subtly, without fanfare. When I

later make a point of watching the Las Vegas nightfall by sitting beside the Luxor's huge outdoor fountain, I too get caught up in the myth of this town's endless, bright days. Sitting among the lights, I hardly notice the sunset when it finally arrives, not even the subsequent quick chill in the air as the natural day darkens. In fact, I only take note of the dusk after I suddenly feel the fountain's spray on my back. I look behind me. Signs posted on lamp posts nearby read: *Luxor Laser and Fountain Show Starts Daily at Dusk.*

Las Vegas has a citywide knack for smoothing over the gaps between day and night, literally and metaphorically. Days, it seems, outnumber nights here. Outlast them, too. Slipping us seamlessly into after-hours with its light, Las Vegas can shut all our nightmares out. Nowhere else in America have I seen whole families by the dozens walking down the sidewalk of a large city such as this—holding hands, taking photos, drinking, laughing, and buying souvenirs at 4 A.M.

To come to Las Vegas is to gorge one's senses to the point of ecstasy. It is a light-happy world in which darkness—spiritually, ethically, and literally—does not exist. All liquor in Las Vegas, for example, is free. All the all-you-can-eat buffets are nearly free. The hotel rooms are practically free. Sunshine's constant. Water's ever ready. Sex is as easy to grab as the escort pamphlets passed out by kids along the Strip. It is the fastest growing city in the United States, and, according to *Money Magazine,* boasts the largest number of college graduates who park cars for a living, earning an estimated $70,000 per year. Ancient Egypt shares a block with medieval Europe, across the street from New York City, beside a little Italian village, a pirate's cove, a circus tent, ancient Rome, modern Paris, Venice, Rio, New Orleans, the Titanic in its glory before "that dark and dreadful night." And all of it is spotlit by theatrical light wizards—from the largest hotel in the world, to the kiosks selling T-shirts. The residents, businesses, and visitors to Las Vegas use almost $800 million worth of electricity every year. And it is this electric light that sets the terms for experience in Vegas. Light sets the stage; we all know our cues.

Tonight, across the street, a man's been wandering among the traffic in the intersection, the busiest four corners in the world. He's not saying anything, just swerving around cars. He's been wandering for a half hour, nearly struck several times. When the cops finally arrive they sit the man down on the curb, take his name, home address, make sure he has a place to sleep tonight, then leave. They don't arrest him or cuff him. They don't do anything about the man because he's done nothing wrong. He isn't drunk, isn't high, isn't mentally deranged. The man's just tired, the cops tell me before they leave. He's a tourist from Europe and hasn't slept in three days—overstimulated by the crowds, the pace, the lights, they say. It's a condition among tourists that's nearly epidemic in this town, known in local precincts as "Vegas Syndrome."

THE SEVENTH DAY

Leaving my room on the eighteenth floor, I overhear two kids outside in the hall daring each other to spit over the railing and hit something below in the hotel atrium.

Because we're so high up and slanting inward, one of the

kids bets the other that a well-aimed spitball would probably fall straight into the Virtualand arcade.

They let one go as I walk past.

It shimmers as it drops—another sparkle among millions—then disappears.

Pthh.

Cheers.

It is time to turn on the light.

The Office of Attractions at the Luxor Hotel is a windowless, one-roomed, attractionless chamber filled with five desks, five women, and a chorus of two-way radios cackling nonstop.

I've got a short at Tut's, sector 1-4-8 . . .

Need a clamp for the barges, over . . .

Fuck, it's hot . . .

Hey, Katie, when's that kid coming for the tour?

This last voice is Jed's, my Luxor light guide, and the only technician in the world who is allowed near the hotel's big beam. He was hand-picked for the job by designer Joshua Thomas and wooed away from Universal Studios in Florida. Among Las Vegas lighting technicians—among the men and women who flip switches to turn volcanoes on; among those who illuminate fountains that dance to Frank Sinatra; among the programmers of computers that hurl fireballs at pirate ships, that spotlight roaring lions, that keep Christmas lights twinkling on imported pine trees—Jed wields the most powerful light switch in town.

"Sorry there," he says, wiping his hand before shaking mine. "We're short some men these days so I'm doing a lot of grimy work. You set with the bathroom?"

I look at him.

"There's no place to take a piss up there so you'll have to come all the way back down. And it's a bitch of a climb when you gotta go."

Negotiating a shortcut through the casino in his khaki Luxor jumpsuit, Jed leads the way like a guide through the Sahara.

Getting there is not easy.

Turned down after my first request to see the Luxor's light, I changed my name and tried again with the public relations office. I had to send them proof that I was a physics student researching light. I had to fax a prospectus. Had to sign a waiver. Had to pledge not to brag to my school peers that I got to visit the light. The power of the light is secret, they warned. But it is hard to imagine why. Most journals of lighting design have profiled Joshua Thomas, and most have already published diagrams of his lighting techniques. At this point, the light's only remaining secret lies in PR mystique.

I follow Jed. The inclinator takes us up thirty floors, deep into the crotch of Luxor. The highest guest floor angles so tightly toward the apex that there is only enough room for the Presidential Suite.

We go higher.

Through a secure door we scale a stairwell, climb two more floors, open another door, and enter the bones of the building.

At this height, we could be among the ghosts of pharaohs. I look around. The walls are merely sky, a glass shell of the building only partially covered by insulation and wiring. The floor isn't solid, it's a catwalk of metal grids below which everything I know exists. We are that high now: in the eye of the pyramid, the sealed-off part from which even the pharaoh is kept. It is a place that clanks with the steely cold ugliness of how this pharaoh's myth—like any myth—is made.

Yes. There are ghosts in this place.

But Jed points farther up.

A ladder bracketed to the wall soars through the grid above it, and we are climbing. Ninety degrees. One floor, another floor, onto a grid to rest—one more. Finally, Jed grabs my hand, pulling me onto a concrete island suspended below the apex by a matrix of steel and magic.

"This is it," he says.

I take a moment to catch my breath. I lower my head to wait out dizziness. When my eyes clear, what I first see is a plaque.

"Oh, that," Jed says, nodding to the floor where the plaque's embedded in concrete. "It's for two guys who ate it while they were building the place. One of them was crushed by a crane, the other took a nosedive down the air shaft. From here all the way to the ground. Took him away in Baggies."

There is glass, steel, plastic, light. Four giant vents in the four corners below the peak are vacuuming heat out of the room. The light, when we turn it on, will be hot enough to melt itself.

"It's not because of the light per se, it's just all these power crates," he says. Jed rests his hand on one of the large black boxes in the room. They're what fuel the fire, they're what light the lights. Plural. *Lights.* It is not one giant lightbulb, as I had been trying to imagine it till now. Instead, the brightest light in the world is comprised of forty-five separate lamps, each the size of a searchlight, arranged in three concentric circles, and all aimed at the peak.

Xenotech, a lighting company, worked with Joshua Thomas to customize the system. Each bulb costs $1,500. Each reflector is $1,000. Every unit—lamp, generator, bulb, etc.—costs $32,000. To merely outfit the Luxor with its lighting equipment alone cost nearly $2 million.

"When one of these babies bursts, the suits downstairs go shit-crazy," Jed says.

The lights, called Xenotech 7000s, are considered in the industry the finest equipment around. Indeed, impressed by the 7000s' performance at Luxor, the Community Christian parish of Kansas City, Missouri, finally exhumed its church's original 1940 blueprints, completing the dream of its maker, Frank Lloyd Wright, by capping their flat-roofed building with what Wright called "a steeple of light." Fifty years later. It took that long to find a lighting system bright enough to create Wright's effect, church officials say. Now they eagerly point out in a new parish brochure that their church shares a steeple with the world-famous Luxor.

The Xenotechs are bright because they're filled with xenon gas, an innovation in lightbulbs pioneered by Joshua. The benefits of the gas for lighting are aesthetic. The drawbacks of the gas, however, are deadly. Every lamp of xenon running at full power is under approximately seven atmospheres of pressure. Everyday pressure on earth is three.

"When these things explode, you don't want to be around," Jed says.

He often has been.

"It's not the heat, it's not the cold. They're just unstable fuckers. The older they get the more likely they'll explode. But some of them just go off sitting in the cabinet, in their boxes, not even opened."

Jed points.

DANGER FLAMMABLE EXPLOSIVE on the red closet door.

"When they first told me they wanted me to wear a bomb suit while I was working up here, I was like, 'What the fuck?'" Jed says. "But then I saw one of them go off, like thirty feet away, and I'm not taking any chances, man, you know?"

Grabbing his dick, Jed sounds sincere.

"You got to watch yourself up here."

How vulnerable is a dick in the desert? Just last night, during dinner at the Pyramid Café, I overheard two waitresses gossiping about one of the dancers in the dinner show.

"Liz said he complained about some safety problem, like having to dance around all that fire and stuff," one of the waitresses confided in another. "Honestly, though? Liz says it's just 'cause he wouldn't wear this little loincloth thing. So they fired him."

A towel boy at the pool: "You didn't hear it from me, but there's this rumor flying around that the place has sank like six inches since they built it. They gave me the choice to work inside for twice the cash, but no way I'm gonna be in there when that thing comes down."

How vulnerable is a pyramid in the desert? Last year, the Luxor's parent company's stock dropped 2¼ points on the

New York Stock Exchange. And since Luxor's opening in '94, the stock has plummeted a total of 35 points, from 42⅛ to 7⅞. Even standard weekly room rates have dropped—from $79 to $40 a night.

"They just can't compete," says Jed. "Sure we've got this light, but people after a while are like, 'Whoopee. Big deal.' They just opened this hotel called New York, New York, right next door. They got replicas of the Brooklyn Bridge, the Statue of Liberty, the Empire State Building, all that stuff. At night, I've heard they're planning on having this free show outside where a huge King Kong head will pop up behind the hotel and start reaching out with this huge fist. We're just not going to be able to compete with that. All that fire and smoke and the sound effects? We're just a light, man. I mean, big shit."

The brightest light in the world thrums quietly beside me. A god in its lonely temple, its lonely watchman nearby. I look at one of Jed's offerings to the light. On a stretch of duct tape stuck to a lamp, Jed has written: "Pillage list: reflector shot, lens cracked, filter needs new top. . . ." Every lamp, I notice, has one.

"It's not easy," he says. "They're running us ragged. We've dropped from fifteen guys in our department down to nine. They've got me working on the fucking talking camels in the lobby."

Jed is thinking seriously about giving up and heading back to Florida. But when he thinks about the good life he has going in Las Vegas, its lights like no others, his $25 an hour, his house in a brand-new patrolled development, it's hard. Since settling into his office just below the desert clouds, Jed has watched five new giant hotels, erected out of dust, slowly dust themselves off, and slowly tower above him. He has since been wooed by the tallest.

The highest building west of the Mississippi, the Stratosphere Hotel, now stands at the far end of the Strip from the Luxor. It is crowned by a roller coaster, a revolving restaurant, a weather station monitoring wind, and lights: lights that seem so close to the clouds they're like the sunrise, the sunset, a storm threatening with awesome colors the tiny valley below. Jed looks up—the air exploding around him like ancient, rotting artifacts.

He's still at the Luxor, with black-marker scrawl on one of the steel beams in the peak—"I survived the Luxor light 4/4/94"—mocking him from the shadows.

"What's that date?" I ask.

"Oh," he says. "That's the date they dimmed it."

Citing further budget restraints, the Luxor Hotel's parent company, Circus, Circus Incorporated, ordered 15 of the light's 45 lamps to be permanently cut off. The light's strength was dimmed from 315,000 to 210,000 watts per hour.

"I don't even think it's the brightest light anymore," Jed says. "It's a scam, really. They open with all this brouhaha, 'the brightest light,' la-di-da. And of course they start getting people coming to Vegas who are telling their travel agents, 'We want to stay where the light is! Which one has the light?' Little do they know the light's not half as bright as it should be. I go home and look up and I'm like, 'Where is it?' It sucks, man. You know? 'Cause all they think about is selling those rooms. They don't care about the light. It's just a big dollar sign to them. And Josh? I mean, I'm sure he's a cool guy and all, but he just gets his big fat check, you know? He just gets his check and then that's it—see ya! Nobody really cares about this thing.

"But me? I left my job to come here. My family. I left everything. I wanted to work on the brightest light in the world, you know? *The Brightest Light!* I mean, shit, man, this thing rules! Now I go into a bar . . . and people know. They know, man. They can tell the light's not as bright as it used to be. And the chicks used to love it! I'd say I was the guy that turned the light on and . . . BANG! Now I overhear someone talking about the light and it's like I don't even hear them. I just go around telling people I work on the little amusement rides or something. You know? Just anything."

Hundreds of feet below us, there is still a world that relies on Jed. In the tunnels beneath the Luxor, dozens of people dash past one another in tuxedos and gowns, in capes and loincloths, in jewels, tiaras, and headdresses. A circus awaits its spot. When the beam is turned on, the whole hotel will be cued for the night: younger, beautiful, refreshed staff come on; menus change; dealers raise the minimum bets per table.

A crowd below us outside the Luxor has also probably gathered by now. The daily igniting of Luxor's light is still an attraction for many. Every evening after dusk, for a full fifteen minutes, a laser show precedes the lighting. The giant yellow stucco sphinx that reclines above the hotel carport awakes from its daylight siesta, blinking golden lasers at the crowd. The lagoon beside the sidewalk churns, shirrs, and seethes into a screen of mist. Lasers from a rockbed project images of a pharaoh. He smiles, clears his throat, and greets the guests with a voice that rattles the palms from which it booms. "Welcome to the Luxor Hotel . . . ," he says. And then predicts the coming of a blinding light.

Our cue.

NOTES

Doors Number One, Two, Three, Four, Five, Six, and *Seven:* All are taken from the results of a catalogue search in the Library of Congress, Washington, D.C., under the title heading "wonders and of."

*

Round Trip: To date, the best essay to capture the aspirations of the generation that built Hoover Dam is, in my opinion, Joan Didion's elegant "At the Dam" (*The White Album,* 1979). This essay is dedicated to that one.

*

Martha Graham, Audio Description Of: This one is for Deborah.

*

Flat Earth Map: An Essay: "An essay that becomes a lyric is an essay that has killed itself" is a very loose translation of a line from Camus's *Lyrical and Critical Essays,* which itself is borrowed from Plutarch's introduction to his series of essays on aphorisms.

*

Hall of Fame: In the process of writing this series I visited 79 halls of fame. There are approximately 2,921 more in the United States.

The epigraph to this essay is by Geoffrey Chaucer, who left his epic poem "Hous of Fame" incomplete in 1378 or 1379—scholars aren't entirely certain which. Nevertheless, this was long before his death on October 25, 1400. Why Chaucer left this manuscript incomplete is unknown.

The first hall in the essay, "Hall of Fame of You," refers to pre-Hellenic Greek *kouroi,* full-sized marble representations of Apollo, who, in pre-Platonic Greek thinking, was the ideal manifestation of the human body and mind. Sculpturally speaking, however, *kouroi* are important because they represent a link between the influence of stylized Egyptian aesthetics on early Greek sculpture and the climax of natural form during the classical "Golden Age" in Greek art, a historical transition captured best in the otherwise rigid *kouros* by the slight displacement of one of the figure's feet beyond the space of the body, into the space of the world. "A step toward the future of human civilization," as one Getty docent explained on a tour. Authentic *kouri* are rare, and thus hot items among collectors. Due to the controversy surrounding its authenticity, the Getty's *kouros* has been removed from exhibit. The first line in the fifth section of "You" borrows its syntax from James Tate.

"Hall of Fame of Me" takes place, in my mind, at the Cambridge, Massachusetts, branch of the California Cryo Bank, a sperm depository. As a student I was "employed" at the Bank from 1995 to 1998.

"Let us cross over the river and rest under the shade of the trees" in "Living History Hall of Fame, ii" are the last words spoken by Stonewall Jackson.

Flax, as described in "Museum of American Frontier Culture and Hall of Fame," is the earliest known fiber to have been cultivated by humans for the purposes of weaving fabric. Leslie Little's excellent study "City in the Distance" argues entertainingly and brilliantly that the great American migration West would never have happened as quickly, completely, nor as successfully if it were not for flax in the *East*.

The Bristlecone Pine Trees referred to in "Oldest Hall of Fame on Earth" have been known to live 4,900 years, about 3,500 more than the oldest redwoods. I would like my friend Joanna to know that I will always love her.

E Clampus Vitus in "August Hall of Fame: An Afterword on Heat" is a benevolent, secret, all-male society headquartered somewhere in the American West. Its two primary stated goals as an organization are 1) "to promote unique landmarks in the American West" and 2) "to support widows and orphans." ECV, as it is called, recently placed a plaque at the foot of the World's Tallest Thermometer dedicated to Daniel Fahrenheit. The National Park Service has since removed it.

The fact that Mercury's sandals did not leave footprints is interesting, I think, because the same was said of Jesus.

These halls are for Jorie.

*

Notes toward the making of a whole human being . . . : Technically speaking, a periodic sentence does not have to be long. In fact, a *periodic* is defined as a "rounded sentence," etymologically deriving from the Greek word for "cycle," *periodikós*. But traditionally a periodic is characterized by an elaborate system of clauses often nested one within the other, like Chinese boxes. For purely practical reasons, the subject and verb in a periodic sentence often serve as bookends to the sentence, providing a rudimentary syntactic vessel into which the sentence's more intricate complex and compound clauses can be poured. Primarily a rhetorical device for use in oratory, the classical Ciceronian periodic sentence is designed to hold a large crowd in suspense as to the point being made in the speech at hand— effectively holding the audience captive, literally, as it awaits the final key verb that will unlock the sentence's meaning. There is, in my mind, a touch of desperation in the use of a periodic sentence.

I was a student at Deep Springs in 1995.

*

Collage History of Art, by Henry Darger. This essay takes liberties with the facts of Henry's life. It also appropriates work from other texts in the spirit of Henry's own love of collage.

"He commenced the long struggle . . . ," for example, is actually thought to be a line by Gertrude Stein in reference to Picasso's *Les Demoiselles d'Avignon.*

"One must have a good memory . . ." is from *Human, All Too Human* by Friedrich Nietzsche.

"Prophets of Nature, we to them will speak . . ." is from *The Prelude* by William Wordsworth.

"Could the flap of a butterfly's wings . . ." is from an address to the American Association for the Advancement of Science in 1979 by Edward Lorenz.

"When you're all alone . . ." is from Leonardo da Vinci's *Notebooks.*

"Who is worthy to open the book . . ." is from St. John's *Revelation.*

"That which *is* grows . . ." is from *On the Natural Faculties* by Galen.

"A crowd is not company, and faces are but a gallery . . ." is from Francis Bacon's essay "On Friendship."

"Surely the heart must break . . ." is from Henry Darger's journals, unpublished as of yet.

*

And There Was Evening and There Was Morning: Due to legal concerns that I don't quite understand, all of the names in this work have been changed, except, of course, for "Luxor" and "Vegas."

This essay is dedicated to my grandfather, Sam, who passed away while I was writing it, and who urged me, a few days prior, to find myself a religion.

Acknowledgments

Essays are costly things.

I'm grateful for the financial assistance of my grandmother Lil, who collected several dozen 2-liter ginger ale bottles filled with dimes so that I could make my first trip to Las Vegas. My other grandmother, Flo, graciously invited me to live on her golf course in Naples so that I could write for six months in green. Additional aid came from a Maine State Arts grant and an award from the Iowa Arts Foundation.

The MacDowell Colony, Villa Montalvo, Djerassi, and The Ucross Foundation fed me, housed me, introduced me to new friends, and allowed me the luxury of thinking out loud.

For three years the University of Iowa Writers' Workshop and the Department of English's Program in Nonfiction patiently allowed me to explore the terrain between poems and essays.

The Paris Review first published "Living History Hall of Fame, i"; *The Gettysburg Review* published "Flat Earth Map: An Essay"; *Colorado Review* published "Oldest Hall of Fame on Earth" and "Hall of Fame of Me"; *The Georgia Review* published "Martha Graham, Audio Description Of"; *Ploughshares* published "Museum

of American Frontier Culture and Hall of Fame"; *Witness* published "American Police Hall of Fame"; *Fourth Genre* published
"Hall of Fame of Us" and "Hall of Fame of Them"; *The Journal*
published "U.S. Astronaut Hall of Fame"; *Jubilat* published
"Living History Hall of Fame, ii," "Big Daddy's Drag Racing Hall
of Fame," and "Magic Hall of Fame"; *Creative Nonfiction* published "Round Trip"; and *The North American Review* published
"And There Was Evening and There Was Morning."

These people read drafts: Mary Caponegro, Anne Carson, Carol de
Saint Victor, Paul Diehl, Mark Doty, Forrest Gander, Jim Galvin,
Jorie Graham, David Hamilton, Mary Hussmann, Sara Levine,
Judith Kitchen, Joanna Klink, Wayne Koestenbaum, Susan Mitchell,
Honor Moore, Peg Peoples, Scott Russell Sanders, Richard Selzer,
Bob Shachocis, David Shields, Tom Simmons, Deborah Tall, David
Weiss, Terry Tempest Williams, C.D. Wright, and Dean Young.
They have my love.

A Note about the Author

JOHN D'AGATA received MFAs in both nonfiction and poetry from the Iowa Writers' Workshop and has since taught at universities in New York, Wyoming, California, and Maine. He is the editor of *The Next American Essay* and editor of lyric essays for the *Seneca Review.*

The text of this book was typeset in 12/16 Adobe Garamond, a typeface drawn by Robert Slimbach and based on type cut by Claude Garamond in the sixteenth century. This book was set in type by Stanton Publication Services, St. Paul, Minnesota, and manufactured by Sheridan Books on acid-free paper.

Graywolf Press is a not-for-profit, independent press. The books we publish include poetry, literary fiction, essays, and cultural criticism. We are less interested in best-sellers than in talented writers who display a freshness of voice coupled with a distinct vision. We believe these are the very qualities essential to shape a vital and diverse culture.

Thankfully, many of our readers feel the same way. They have shown this through their desire to buy books by Graywolf writers; they have told us this themselves through their e-mail notes and at author events; and they have reinforced their commitment by contributing financial support, in small amounts and in large amounts, and joining the "Friends at Graywolf."

If you enjoyed this book and wish to learn more about Graywolf Press, we invite you to ask your bookseller or librarian about further Graywolf titles; or to contact us for a free catalog; or to visit our award-winning web site that features information about our forthcoming books.

We would also like to invite you to consider joining the hundreds of individuals who are already "Friends of Graywolf" by contributing to our membership program. Individual donations of any size are significant to us: they tell us that you believe that the kind of publishing we do *matters*. Our web site gives you many more details about the benefits you will enjoy as a "Friend of Graywolf"; but if you do not have online access, we urge you to contact us for a copy of our membership brochure.

www.graywolfpress.org

Graywolf Press
2402 University Avenue, Suite 203
Saint Paul, MN 55114
Phone: (651) 641-0077
Fax: (651) 641-0036
E-mail: wolves@graywolfpress.org